Sacred
Rituals
at
Home

Sacred
Rituals
at
Home

 A GODSFIELD BOOK

Library of Congress Cataloging-in-Publication
Data Available

10 9 8 7 6 5 4 3 2 1

Originally published under the title
Rituals for Sacred Living

PUBLISHED IN 2000 BY
Sterling Publishing Company, Inc.
387 Park Avenue South,
New York, N.Y. 10016

© 1999 Godsfield Press
Text © 1999 Jane Alexander

Designed for Godsfield Press by The Bridgewater Book Company

Studio Photography: Ian Parsons, Guy Ryecart,
Walter Gardiner, Zul Mukhida
Illustrations: Sarah Young
Picture Research: Vanessa Fletcher

Special thanks go to Kay Macmullan *for help with photography*

Jane Alexander asserts the moral right
to be identified as the author of this work.

DISTRIBUTED IN CANADA BY
Sterling Publishing
c/o Canadian Manda Group, One Atlantic Avenue,
Suite 105, Toronto, Ontario, Canada M6K 3E7

DISTRIBUTED IN AUSTRALIA BY
Capricorn Link (Australia) Pty Ltd.
P. O. Box 6651, Baulkham Hills,
Business Centre, NSW 2153, Australia

Every effort has been made to ensure that all the information in this book is accurate.
However, due to differing conditions, tools, and individual skills, the publisher cannot be responsible
for any injuries, losses, and other damages that may result from the use of the information in this book.

Printed and bound in Hong Kong

Sterling ISBN 0-8069-7159-2

CONTENTS

WHAT IS SACRED LIVING?

S acred living is to live and work in complete harmony with yourself, with your friends, family, and co-workers, and with your environment. This involves self-awareness, acceptance, and love.

What inspires us and guides us to live in a sacred way? However secular we may consider ourselves and our society to be, there is still a deep need for a sense of the divine – a yearning for a feeling of belonging.

Beyond us all is a greater force that longs to connect with us and that we yearn to embrace. Whether we call this force God, Goddess, Great Spirit, or any other name, most of us have experienced the feeling or conviction that there is someone or something greater than us that pulls us toward the sacred. It seems almost as though our psyches are programmed to search for meaning in our lives.

MANY SPIRITUAL PATHS

There are many different paths to the sacred. Some people find their sacred path and inspiration fulfilled by faith in organized religion. They find peace and purpose in the comfort of church, mosque, temple, or synagogue liturgy and the familiarity of rituals that date back hundreds or thousands of years. Others seek to connect with the ancient Earth-centered religions and are rediscovering Paganism, Shamanism, Druidism, and other nature-based paths. Still more find themselves trying to connect to Spirit in new and different ways – seeking angels, channeling spirit guides, and gaining a sense of the sacred that is not bounded by prescribed traditions. Finally, some people do not have a fixed belief system or a rigid prescription for connecting with the sacred – they just know there is something more to life than waking, working, and sleeping.

INSPIRATION IN EVERYTHING

Native American culture teaches the concept of the Medicine Walk, in which everything you come across – whether a person, animal, stone, or cloud – is believed to have a special meaning, or a message, for you and your life.

OPENING YOURSELF TO INSPIRATION

◆ Get in touch with the wonder of your body. Stretch every muscle. Lie down and become aware of how your body connects with the earth. Tap your bones and hear and feel the difference in each part of your body.

FEEL YOURSELF
CONNECTING TO
THE EARTH

Try to visualize yourself as a stone.

Try to visualize yourself as a leaf.

◆ Pick up a stone: feel it, smell it, look at it, taste it. Really get to know the stone. Wonder at its age and history. Try to imagine being that stone. Now pick up a leaf and do the same. How do they differ? How do your feelings differ?

Some Native American teachers say that if we are truly aware, we see the whole of life as a Medicine Walk and pay attention to every "teacher" we meet. Interestingly, modern psychologists are beginning to say much the same: that whatever affects our psyche, it does so for a specific purpose.

Once you become open to the sacred, you will find inspiration everywhere: in the wonder of your own body, in the beauty of nature, in the joy of simple pleasures, even in the apparent "ugliness" of modern urban living. Start to become more aware, more open to nature and the beauty of everyday living, and the sacred will enter your life.

WHAT ARE RITUALS?

In this crazy, modern world, many of us are seeking to find a way of making life more spiritual. We are looking for something to put us in touch, even if just for a moment, with the divine. We want our lives to have more meaning, more purpose, more beauty. Rituals can help us achieve this.

The aim of this book is to help you to bring ritual back into your life. Not as boring duty, but as a vibrant part of spiritual life. Even the smallest of ceremonies and rituals can give meaning to everyday life and allow us to connect with each other, with our own psyches, with the transitions and passages of our lives. Above all, rituals can reconnect us to the spiritual world.

THE NEED FOR RITUAL

Good rituals are vital to our psychological and spiritual health. A "good ritual" can be any ceremony that has personal and transcendental meaning. You must be able to connect at this profound level, or your rituals will always feel banal or lacking some some vital ingredient – they will irritate rather than comfort. If your rituals have meaning, they will enhance the quality of your life.

A good ritual can soothe the soul and balance the psyche. It offers us a chance to express our emotions, to understand our feelings, and to come to terms with our place in the universe. Above all, a good ritual enables us to enjoy special moments with ourselves and with others, and connects us with the divine.

TOP LEFT: Nature is a vital source of spiritual strength and connection with the divine.
BOTTOM LEFT: Simple rituals and ceremonies can sacralize even the most hectic urban lifestyle.

WHAT CONSTITUTES A RITUAL?

What does the word "ritual" mean to you? A boring duty or a dull liturgy? Perhaps an arduous ordeal? We tend to think of rituals as elaborate ceremonies with rigid rules and regulations, conducted in special vestments, and surrounded by ornate trappings. We may imagine rituals to be set in stone, ossified through the years so that they become dreary and meaningless. But the fundamental purpose of a ritual is simply to connect with Spirit; it is a way of making a space, however small, for the sacred in your life. A ritual can be as simple or as complex as you wish. Throughout this book we have used props such as crystals, oils, candles, and natural objects, but they serve solely to focus the mind. At its most basic, a ritual needs no more than you and your intent.

MAKING RITUALS YOUR OWN

In order to bring meaning into your rituals, you should aim to make them your own. Use the ideas in this book as a springboard, not as a prescription. Follow your intuition. For example, feel free to choose your own incenses, herbs, and candle colors – and experiment as much as possible. A good ritual should touch you at the deepest level; it should soothe and calm the soul. If anything jars or feels uncomfortable during your ritual, then you may need to adjust it. Above all, never feel you have to follow any part of a ritual that goes against your spiritual beliefs. These are your rituals: change them or adapt them to suit your own purposes.

A few basic props can help to focus your ritual activities.

THINKING ABOUT RITUAL IN YOUR LIFE

Think about these questions:
◆ What rituals or ceremonies do you follow in your family and what beliefs do they express?
◆ Do your rituals represent what you truly believe, or do you go through the motions to please other people?
◆ Do you and your loved ones celebrate important yearly events such as birthdays and wedding anniversaries, or do they simply slide by with little notice? How about key events such as retirement or graduation?

The way you mark key anniversaries and events reveals a lot about your sense of the sacred.

THE FUN OF RITUAL

Rituals should never be boring or something you think of as a chore. Rituals can give us a chance to be creative and playful, and to explore the meaning of our lives in a joyful way. They can also empower us and allow us to live our lives to the full. They are all about rediscovering our sense of fun, and the sheer joy of being alive.

ENJOY YOUR RITUALS

The best rituals are those that you enjoy so much they simply have to become part of your everyday life. How do you feel about the rituals you already incorporate into your life: family birthdays, Sunday dinners, or vacations perhaps? Do you look forward to them, or do you secretly dread them? Are they happy occasions for you and your loved ones, or are they a source of tension? If your rituals are too rigid, if they have stayed the same for years, it may be time to change them. If your rituals do not work for you,

Children take straightforward pleasure in ritual gatherings.

change them. Rituals should grow and evolve all the time; they should also be personal and relevant to your life.

A child is born with an inbuilt sense of the magic and wonder of life and the sacred. As children we are open to possibilities, fantasies, and realms of the imagination that gradually become stifled through the socializing process. As adults it is possible for us to tap into that sacred space, the space of creativity, dreams, and imagination, and to rediscover our sense of wonder in life.

• What were your favorite childhood games? Can you try playing any of them now?

• Did you have any imaginary friends? What games of the imagination did you play?

• Were there any places that were special, magical, or sacred for you as a child?

We need to rekindle a childlike sense of the wonder of life.

HUNTING FOR TREASURE

If you have any problems bringing your childhood sense of fun and play into adult life, try creating a Treasure Map. This simple technique is remarkably powerful. By putting your desires into a visual display, it works deeply on an unconscious level and can often produce surprising results.

Take a large sheet of paper, a selection of magazines, a pair of scissors, and some glue.

Look through the magazines for images that sum up fun, joy, and sacredness for you. It could be someone meditating peacefully, or a child hunting for shells on a beach.

Cut out these pictures and paste them onto the sheet of paper. You may be surprised at the pictures you choose; you may also find that they give you some unusual inspiration or guidance.

Put a photograph of yourself in the center of the collage, and position it where you will see it every day. You may discover that a sense of fun and inspiration comes into your life – as if by magic.

Your collage of sacredness will be a source of inspiration.

Gather together images that reflect your own sense of the beauty of life.

MINDFULNESS MEDITATION

Mindfulness is a simple technique that can be used to improve your awareness in seconds. It is meditation brought up to date, honed to slot into the most frenetic Western life. It teaches you how to listen to your mind and body, and allows you to reconnect with your Self and the world around you at any given moment.

The method shown here was pioneered by Jon Kabat-Zinn of the Stress Reduction Clinic at the University of Massachusetts Hospital, who found that mindfulness can help all manner of physical problems. On an emotional level, it can lessen feelings of anxiety and depression, and enables us to understand our true feelings and motivations.

Mindfulness meditation also works perfectly for spiritual purposes: it allows us to bring small amounts of awareness and sacredness into the busiest working day.

BELOW: Modern lifestyles frequently lead to a dulling of our awareness of our surroundings, whether through monotonous routine or frantic activity.

ALLOWING TIME FOR MINDFULNESS

Mindfulness is a simple technique. At its very basic level, it involves stopping whatever you are doing and becoming aware of the moment. The easiest way to do it is to focus on your breathing, and gently let go of any stray thoughts or worries that emerge. Whether it's just for five minutes or even five seconds at first, just breathe and let go. Give yourself permission to allow this moment to be exactly as it is and allow yourself to be exactly as you are without altering your perception in any way. Try to build up to 45 minutes of mindfulness a day, but even a few minutes will make a great difference.

RIGHT: Take time out to make contact with your inmost self.

RECONNECTING THROUGHOUT THE DAY

♦ Start each day with mindfulness. Practice the Welcome the Day ritual (see pages 20–21) with mindfulness.

♦ Stop, sit down, and become aware of your breathing once in a while throughout the day. It can be for five minutes or even five seconds. Just breathe and let go, and allow yourself to be exactly as you are.

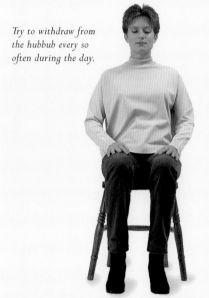

Try to withdraw from the hubbub every so often during the day.

♦ Use your mindfulness time to contemplate what you really want from life. Ask yourself questions such as "Who am I?", "Where am I going?", "If I could choose a path now, in which direction would I head?", "What do I truly love?". You don't have to come up with answers, just persist in asking searching questions.

Focus on simple physical sensations and make them occasions of mindfulness.

♦ Use ordinary occasions to become mindful. When you are in the shower, really feel the water on your skin instead of losing yourself in thought. When you eat, really taste your food. Notice how you feel when the phone rings.

♦ Practice being kind to yourself. As you sit and breathe, invite a sense of self-acceptance and cherishing to arise in your heart. If it starts to go away, gently bring it back. Imagine you are being held in the arms of a loving parent, and that you are completely accepted and completely loved.

♦ Try lying down on the floor once a day and stretching your body mindfully, if only for three or four minutes. Stay in touch with your breathing and listen to what your body has to tell you.

Lying down on the floor allows you to refocus yourself.

CHAPTER ONE

TIME MANAGEMENT

WE MAY WANT TO BRING THE SACRED INTO EVERYDAY LIFE, BUT HOW CAN WE FIND THE TIME TO DO IT? WE LEAD SUCH BUSY, FRANTIC LIVES, IT CAN BE HARD ENOUGH TO FIND TIME FOR THE SHEER PRACTICAL NECESSITIES OF LIFE, WITHOUT HAVING TO MAKE MORE TIME TO LOOK FOR THE SACRED. BUT RITUALS CAN TAKE MINUTES, NOT HOURS, AND THERE ARE PLENTY OF PRACTICAL WAYS TO HELP YOU FIND TIME TO INCORPORATE THEM INTO EVERYDAY LIFE.

However difficult it may seem, if you want to bring the sacred into your life, you will need to find ways to stretch time. By making time for small rituals, for moments of meditation, for seconds of wonder, you will start to open your heart and soul to wider possibilities. It is not as difficult as it sounds. The rituals in this book are not about high ceremonial, fancy trappings, and pompous litany. They simply nudge us back into the "real" world, the world we have lost in the sheer speed of everyday life.

REDISCOVERING THE REAL

In the preindustrial world when life moved to a slower pace, people felt able to take time in their working day to stop, look, feel, and wonder. A stunning sunset would make them pause and stare. They would notice a tiny flower growing in the most inhospitable of places. They would spare the time to exchange a kindly word with a neighbor or a passer-by. Small things, but they connected our ancestors to a greater world. These things helped them to feel connected – to other people, to their community, to an awe of nature.

We had the same knack as children. Every walk became a voyage of discovery; every contact was imbued with meaning. Fortunately, that skill need not be left behind as we grow up: we can choose to reconnect with the wider world once more. We can recapture the magic, but we need to allow ourselves a little extra time to bring the magic and wonder back into our lives.

Effective time management enables us to find the extra time we need to reconnect with the sacred. It calls for a reassessment of our goals and a reordering of priorities, and allows us to discard any tasks or goals that have outlived their usefulness. Once we have streamlined our responsibilities, and released ourselves from unnecessary chores, we can use the free time we have gained to recapture the inspiration and magic of childhood.

RIGHT: Time need not be a ravenous monster that we have to appease; we can take back time for ourselves through a few simple techniques.

HOW TO FIND TIME

How do you find spare time in a hectic day? The tips on these pages will not only help you to make time, they will also make you feel more confident, more in control, and more on top of your work and everyday commitments. These simple time-management techniques allow you to work more effectively and still have time for yourself and the sacred. Try them and see your life improve almost overnight.

WHAT ARE YOUR PRIORITIES?

How would you feel if you knew that today was your last day on earth? Would you regret not spending more time at work? Would you lament the hours you missed cleaning? It's unlikely. Yet none of us know how much time we have left, so shouldn't we be spending it more carefully?

Take ten minutes to sit down and think about how you would feel if you were to die now. What haven't you done with your life? What would you regret?

The key to managing your time effectively is to have a clear sense of your goals. Where were you five years ago? What were you doing, who were you with, and what were your dreams? And where are you now? Are you stuck in the same place, still doing things you dislike, still seeing people who don't support you with your goals? In order to shift your perception of time, you must first become aware of what you want and what you need from your life.

PLANNING – STEP BY SMALL STEP

Once you know what you want to do, you can concentrate on how to do it. Don't feel you have to overhaul your entire life or make massive changes. If your aim is to incorporate more time for sacredness and ritual in your life, you can start small. Put aside set amounts of time – it could be as much as an hour or as little as five minutes a day – but make a commitment and stick to it.

One classic technique that really works is to spend a few minutes at the end of each day planning the next day's schedule. It need only take five minutes but it

RIGHT: Listing your goals for the day helps you to stay in control of your time.

Caring for children can make life unpredictable, so you need to have some flexibility.

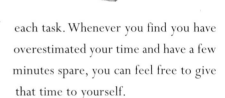

Working from home makes enormous demands on your time-management skills.

could save you hours. Having a clear plan for the day ahead focuses the mind and makes you feel in control, which boosts your energy and your confidence. When you have a clear idea of the tasks and problems for tomorrow, your subconscious brain can start to work ahead of time and produce ideas and solutions – even while you sleep.

Regular tasks can give you anchoring points during the day.

Just before you finish work for the day, ask yourself what scheduled tasks you have for tomorrow. Block them off in your engagement calender. What is the major task you must do tomorrow? Set aside a realistic block of time. Remember to add in any traveling time.

Now make a list of the things you would like to include in your day, such as meditation or small rituals, and allocate a little extra time to

each task. Whenever you find you have overestimated your time and have a few minutes spare, you can feel free to give that time to yourself.

Remember to allow time for your own needs in your planning.

SIMPLE TIME-SAVERS

MANAGING TIME TO HELP US IN SACRED LIVING ISN'T ABOUT TURNING OURSELVES INTO ROBOTS. THE IDEA IS NOT TO SQUEEZE EVERY AVAILABLE MINUTE OUT OF THE DAY, BUT TO TAKE ADVANTAGE OF THE QUIET MOMENTS, TO MAKE CRACKS IN TIME THAT WE CAN USE TO REDISCOVER OUR SACRED SELVES. THE TECHNIQUES ON THESE PAGES ARE INCREDIBLY SIMPLE BUT HIGHLY EFFECTIVE; THEY HELP TO MAKE SACRED SPACE IN EVEN THE MOST HARASSED SCHEDULE.

PRACTICAL MATTERS

• One of the best ways to keep yourself clear and focused is to work on just one thing at a time. Keep only one task on your desk or table at any one time. Clear-desk policies smack of mindless authority but the psychology is absolutely correct. If you are surrounded by clutter and mess, your mind cannot focus properly and you will end up wasting time.

• Another huge ally in the time war is a large wastepaper basket. Open your mail over it. Look at each piece of paper as soon as it arrives and make a firm decision about it. Either deal with it, file it, or throw it away – immediately.

• We waste hours on the telephone. Make a list of essential calls and decide how much time you will

Efficient communication is essential to make the best use of your time.

allow for each one. Stick to it. It can help to bunch all your calls together in a half hour or hour slot. Choose times when you know people will be less likely to chat – just before lunch or going home time!

SCHEDULE TIME FOR YOURSELF

You are important – just as important as deadlines and other people's demands. Start incorporating

A full trash can is a sure sign of effective decision-making.

time for yourself into every day's timetable, and make sure you won't be disturbed during these times. You can use these times for meditation, ritual, setting up an altar (see page 52), planning creative work, or simply for sitting quietly and "refueling". Treat these appointments with yourself just as you would treat appointments with someone else, and only break them if it is absolutely unavoidable.

STRETCH AND REFRESH YOURSELF

Take stretch breaks every hour – make them a habit. Just walk around for a few minutes and you will return refreshed and with your concentration replenished. Also try these simple exercises:

1 Criss-cross: march on the spot, raising your knees up high. As you march, touch each upraised knee with your opposite hand. Try to keep a good rhythm. This has the effect of balancing the left and right hemispheres of the brain, increasing energy and coordination.

3 Ear massage. Simply give both ears a good massage. Start from the lobe and pull and squeeze gently all the way around. This will help to make you feel relaxed yet alert and can be done quietly from the privacy of your own desk.

STEP 3

BELOW: For a simple and quick tonic, try massaging your ears.

STEP 1

ABOVE:
Marching on the spot is a good way of restoring your body's

2 All-over body stretch: stand with your feet shoulder-width apart, and your knees relaxed, not locked. Clasp your hands behind you with your palms facing up. Now take a deep breath in; as you breathe out, bend gently forward and let your head drop loosely to your knees – your clasped hands should reach up behind you. Allow everything to relax: your shoulders, neck, head, and face. Slowly come back up, and repeat if necessary.

STEP 2

ABOVE: An all-over body stretch releases the day's accumulated tensions.

WELCOME THE DAY

THIS LOVELY RITUAL PUTS YOUR MIND INTO A POSITIVE MOOD FOR THE DAY AND REVITALIZES YOUR BODY. DO MAKE TIME FOR THIS RITUAL — EVEN IF IT MEANS GETTING UP A LITTLE EARLIER. THE SALUTE TO THE SUN IS AN ANCIENT YOGA PRACTICE THAT STRETCHES VIRTUALLY EVERY MUSCLE AND ORGAN IN THE BODY. IT ALSO CONNECTS YOU TO THE REVITALIZING ENERGY OF THE RISING SUN, AN AFFIRMATION OF THE REGENERATION OF NATURE AND OUR INDIVIDUAL SOULS.

YOU WILL NEED

◆ A couple of drops of grapefruit essential oil (or any uplifting aromatherapy oil of your choice)

METHOD

1 Before you get out of bed, just relax quietly for a few moments. Say a word of thanks to the Creative Spirit for the gift of life and this new day.

2 Get up and stand in front of a mirror. Smile and affirm that this will be a good day, full of blessings, opportunities, and wonder. Say something like: "I look forward to a wonderful day," or make up an affirmation that is personal to you. If there are difficult meetings or decisions ahead, affirm that you will tackle these with ease: "I will take the challenges of this day in my stride."

3 Now face east and perform the Salute to the Sun. Take it slowly at first (you may wish to record the instructions). In time the routine will become smooth and flowing.

4 Stand upright, and bring your feet together so that your big toes are touching. Your arms should be at

STEP 4

STEP 6

your sides. Relax your shoulders and tuck your chin in slightly. Look straight ahead, not down at your feet. Bring your hands together in front of your chest with your palms together as if you were praying. Exhale deeply.

5 Inhale slowly and deeply while you bring your arms straight up over your head, placing your palms together as you finish inhaling. Gently look up at your hands and

STEP 5

bend backward as far as is comfortable so that you can see your thumbs.

6 Bend forward, exhaling as you do so, until your hands are palms down on the floor, in line with your feet. Tuck your head in toward your knees. It's important not to strain: if necessary bend your knees so that you can reach more comfortably.

STEP 7

7 Without moving your hands, inhale deeply and move your right leg backward as far as possible. Keep your hands and left foot on the ground. Your left knee should be between your arms; your right knee should touch the floor. Bend your head upward.

STEP 8

8 Then, retaining the breath, bring your left leg back, alongside your right leg. Your body should now be in a straight line, with your head looking down.

9 Exhale and lower your body so that your forehead, palms, chest, thighs, knees, and toes touch the floor. Your arms should be bent and your hips raised, as if you were going to do pushups. If your forehead won't reach the floor, use your chin instead.

STEP 9

10 Inhale and push up with your arms to raise your upper body as far back as is comfortable, but keep your body touching the floor from the waist down.

In yoga this is known as the "cobra" position. Keep your elbows slightly bent, and do not strain.

STEP 10

11 Exhale, curl your toes, and lift your back into an arched position.

STEP 11

12 Inhale and return to the position in step 7, but this time move the opposite leg forward so that your right foot is between your arms and your left leg is stretched back.

13 Exhale, and without moving your hands, move your left leg forward and return to the position in step 6.

14 Inhale and you straighten up slowly; raise your arms overhead and bend backward (see step 5).

15 Exhale and return to a comfortable standing position, with your feet together, and your arms by your sides. Look straight ahead.

16 Now put some essential oil on a sponge and take a refreshing shower. Imagine the water cleansing away all negativity and leaving you feeling fresh and ready to greet the day ahead.

LUNCHTIME RENEWAL

YOUR LUNCH BREAK OFFERS THE PERFECT OPPORTUNITY TO RECONNECT WITH THE WIDER WORLD OF THE SACRED. THIS RITUAL IS DECEPTIVELY SIMPLE AND CAN BE EXPANDED OR SIMPLIFIED ACCORDING TO YOUR CIRCUMSTANCES. IT IS BASED ON NATIVE AMERICAN TRADITION AND, IDEALLY, SHOULD BE PERFORMED OUTSIDE IN THE OPEN AIR. HOWEVER, IF YOU CANNOT GET OUTSIDE, YOU CAN STILL ACHIEVE GOOD RESULTS IN YOUR HOME OR OFFICE.

YOU WILL NEED

- *A pinch or two of cornmeal or tobacco*
- *5 drops bergamot and/or lemon essential oil*
- *Tissue or fresh handkerchief*

METHOD

1 Stand or sit quietly. Ground and center yourself (see page 31). Breathe calmly and evenly. Don't force the breath, just be aware of your breathing.

2 Close your eyes and imagine you are standing outside a circle of stones, about five feet in diameter. The stones are different shapes and sizes – some seem to be crystals, glinting in the light. This is the Medicine Wheel of Native American tradition, a sacred space that you can enter at any time for spiritual renewal and relaxation.

3 Imagine taking a step forward so that you are standing in the middle of the circle.

Stand well-balanced, with your feet hip-width apart, and center yourself by breathing calmly.

STEP 1

4 Feel the earth beneath your feet. You are standing firmly on the beautiful body of Mother Earth who will soothe and protect you. Ask Her for Her blessing.

5 Feel (or imagine) the sun on your face, illuminating you. This is the kiss of Father Sky who can uplift you and give you courage. Ask Him for His blessing.

6 You become aware of four great creatures, standing before you, behind you, and to each side. They feel like wonderfully powerful guardian allies, which is exactly what they are.

7 In front of you is the great Eagle Spirit who governs the East. Ask Eagle to give you clear vision, inspiration, and far-sightedness.

8 Behind you is the Bear Spirit who governs the West. Ask Bear to help you discover your True Self and be faithful to your deepest beliefs.

9 To your left is Buffalo who governs the North. Ask Buffalo to grant you wisdom and to make you truly grateful for all the gifts you are given.

10 To your right is Coyote who governs the South. Ask Coyote to give you a child's sense of fun and adventure, so you can approach life as a sacred game.

11 Spend a few moments enjoying being surrounded by these great loving spirits who are there to help you and protect you. Then feel yourself bathed in a clear, bright, white, shining light that washes away all the tiredness and any disillusionment, leaving you feeling fresh, bright, and full of optimism.

12 When you have finished, thank the spirits for their help. Step out of the circle.

13 Leave a pinch of cornmeal or tobacco as a thank-you offering. Slowly become aware of your everyday surroundings. Take out the tissue or handkerchief and put five drops of essential oil on it. Take a few minutes to relax and breathe in the uplifting, energizing scent. You should now be ready to face the rest of your day with joy and vigor.

YOU BECOME AWARE OF FOUR GREAT CREATURES STANDING AROUND YOU

BEAR GOVERNS THE WEST AND WILL HELP YOU IN THE SEARCH FOR YOUR TRUE SELF

COYOTE GOVERNS THE SOUTH AND WILL HELP YOU TO REDISCOVER THE CHILD WITHIN YOU

BUFFALO GOVERNS THE NORTH AND WILL SHOW YOU HOW TO APPRECIATE YOUR BLESSINGS

EAGLE GOVERNS THE EAST AND WILL GIVE YOU INSPIRATION AND CLEAR VISION

RELAXING AFTER WORK

WHENEVER WE'VE SPENT TIME WORKING HARD, IT CAN BE VERY DIFFICULT TO "SWITCH OFF" AFTERWARD. WHEN THIS HAPPENS, WE MAY EITHER CONTINUE IN OUR WORK MODE OR JUST FLOP ON THE SOFA FEELING TIRED AND DRAINED. THIS RITUAL HELPS YOU TO MARK THE TRANSITION FROM WORK TO A STATE OF RELAXATION. IT GIVES YOU A DEEPLY CALM, RELAXED FEELING, YET IT ALSO LEAVES YOU FEELING RENEWED AND INVIGORATED.

YOU WILL NEED

- *A candle and matches*
- *Pen and paper*
- *Geranium essential oil and oil burner*

Pause on the threshold and take your leave of the working day.

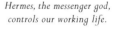
STEP 1

METHOD

1 When you arrive home, before entering your front door pause a moment. In Ancient Greece the threshold of the house was guarded by two divine figures: Hermes and Hestia. Hermes is the god of communication: he presides over our working life. Hestia is the goddess of the home: she can bring a sense of peace and tranquillity to your living space. Imagine these two guardians at the threshold to your home: Hermes facing outward, and Hestia facing inward.

Hermes, the messenger god, controls our working life.

2 Thank Hermes for his help during your busy working day. Take your leave of him and explain you will look forward to seeing him again the next working day. Now take off your shoes and step through the door, being aware that you are crossing an important threshold. (Note: if you work from home, it is worth stepping outside and entering again as if you had been away.) You can put on slippers or

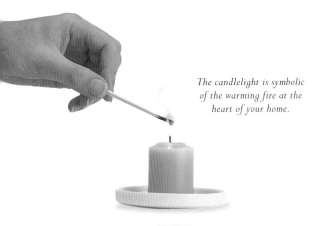

The candlelight is symbolic of the warming fire at the heart of your home.

STEP 3

oil has the power to dissolve tensions and instill a feeling of well-being. Decide how you would like to spend your evening.

The hearth is traditionally the center of the home.

keep your feet bare, but make sure you take off your work shoes. Now greet Hestia: she looks calm and serene and smiles gently to welcome you home.

3 Walk into the center of your home and light a candle. This signifies that you have returned the heart to your home. In Ancient Greece, Hestia was always invoked with a living fire in the hearth.

4 Sit in front of the candle and spend a few moments quietly thinking back over the day. Are there any worries or concerns? Is there anything bothering you? If so, write down your thoughts and make the decision that you will deal with them the next day, with the help of clever, wily Hermes.

5 Now light the oil burner and add a few drops of geranium oil to the water reservoir. Geranium

6 If you are still feeling tense, lie down and focus on your breathing. Be aware of where you are holding tension. Now progressively go through your body, tensing and relaxing each area in turn. Start by concentrating on your scalp and head: tense all the tiny muscles, hold for a few moments, then relax them completely. Continue with your face, neck, chest, arms, hands, abdomen, hips, buttocks, thighs, calves, feet. Lie still and feel the difference.

7 Get up slowly and drink a large glass of fresh water to purify and refresh yourself. Now enjoy the rest of your day.

STEP 5

Using the support of the ground will help you to relax completely.

RELEASE THE MUSCLES OF YOUR SCALP AND HEAD

STEP 6

FEEL THE GROUND BEARING YOU UP

LET YOUR SHOULDERS RELAX

CHAPTER TWO

HOME AS A REFLECTION OF THE SOUL

WHEN WE WALK THROUGH OUR FRONT DOOR, WE SHOULD BE ABLE TO LEAVE THE STRESSES AND STRAINS OF THE OUTSIDE WORLD BEHIND. A HOME SHOULD PROVIDE US WITH A SANCTUARY FOR THE SOUL, A HAVEN FOR THE SENSES. IT SHOULD BE AN OASIS OF CALM AND SECURITY, A PLACE WHERE WE CAN BE TOTALLY OURSELVES, WITH NO NEED FOR PRETENSE. THIS CHAPTER LOOKS AT SIMPLE BUT EFFECTIVE WAYS TO TRANSFORM OUR HOMES INTO PLACES OF SPIRITUAL RENEWAL.

THE IMPORTANCE OF HOME

Our homes are important to our souls because they represent our own world in miniature. When we feel safe and comfortable in our homes, we feel more able to deal with the ups and downs of the outside world. Deep in our psyches, we recognize that a house or apartment is far more than just a place to eat and sleep.

DOES YOUR HOME REFLECT YOUR SOUL?

How do you feel when you walk into your home? Does a wonderful sense of peace and happiness descend on you, or do you feel irritated and stressed the moment you step through the door? If your home truly reflects your soul, you will feel full of well-being when you are there – completely safe, relaxed, and energized. If you constantly feel depressed, jumpy, nervous, or exhausted in your home, it is not serving the needs of your soul.

THE PSYCHOLOGY OF THE HOME

It's important to realize that we all have different needs. One way of understanding our homes and ourselves is to look at the four personality types defined by psychologist Carl Jung.

SENSATION: These people rely on their senses and prefer practical, well-functioning homes to stylish appearances. They crave tidiness and a sense of order.

INTUITION: Intuitive types are highly sensitive to atmosphere and the flow of subtle energy. They often create beautiful but impractical surroundings. Their homes can seem eccentric.

THINKING: Thinking people prefer ideas to objects. As long as they can put their books somewhere, they are happy. They can be absent-minded, and barely notice clutter building up.

FEELING: Feeling people are the world's natural interior designers. They want their homes to look and feel good, to others as well as themselves. They prefer the latest fashions and designs.

THINKING ABOUT
YOUR SOUL HOME

FOR SOME OF US A SOUL HOME IS A COUNTRY COTTAGE OR CABIN, SIMPLE AND FULL OF RUSTIC CHARM. FOR OTHERS, THE EPITOME OF SOUL IS AN INNER-CITY LOFT, VIBRATING TO THE CONSTANT HUM OF HUMANITY. THERE IS NO SINGLE FORMULA FOR A SOUL HOME: IT COULD BE A HUGE MANSION OR A ONE-ROOM APARTMENT. BUT BEFORE WE CAN BEGIN TO IMBUE OUR HOMES WITH SOUL, WE NEED TO CLARIFY OUR IDEAS ABOUT WHAT CONSTITUTES A SOUL HOME.

BUILDING A
PICTURE OF HOME

There are many ways to discover which elements would make a soul home for you. Try these:

The memory of a favorite place can reveal aspects of what you crave from a soul home.

• Think back to the homes you lived in as a child. What were they like? What did you like about them? Are there any elements of those homes that fill you with nostalgia?
• Now consider the places you have stayed in and loved. A particular vacation cottage perhaps? A hotel or retreat center? What did they have in common?

Often it will not be the physical structure of the place but a feeling. Try to pinpoint the feeling: could you reproduce it in your own home?
• Get out some paints and paper and try painting an image of your soul home. It need not be representative, it could just be a series of colors or shapes. Don't think too much about it, just paint and see what happens. You might like to try painting with your nondominant hand, or with your eyes shut. Then sit back and try to see what your intuition says about the images you have created.
• Take out your magazines again and make a collage, as you may have done in the introduction to this book (see page 11). This time, look for images that spell "home" to you. You may be surprised by what your subconscious mind craves.

Try to connect with your subconscious by painting your images of home.

TALKING TO YOUR HOME

It sounds crazy, but talking to your home can be a wonderfully enlightening – and delightful – process. Every home has a spirit or soul of its own. If you take the time to listen, you can learn a lot about both your home and your inner self.

STEP 1

1 Choose a time when you are alone and feel relaxed. Go to the center of your home and sit quietly for a few moments. Close your eyes and pay attention to your breathing. You may like to light some incense or burn a little essential oil.

2 When you feel calm and centered, greet your home and its attendant spirit. You might apologize for not having given it recognition before. Then ask it for some enlightenment. You might ask your home what it would like. Some homes crave loving care and attention. Others want a more peaceful atmosphere, especially if there is family bickering and fighting.

3 Ask your house for its help in achieving your spiritual aims. Ask how it can help you find the sacred in your life.

4 Thank your home for its help and promise that you will consult it in the future.

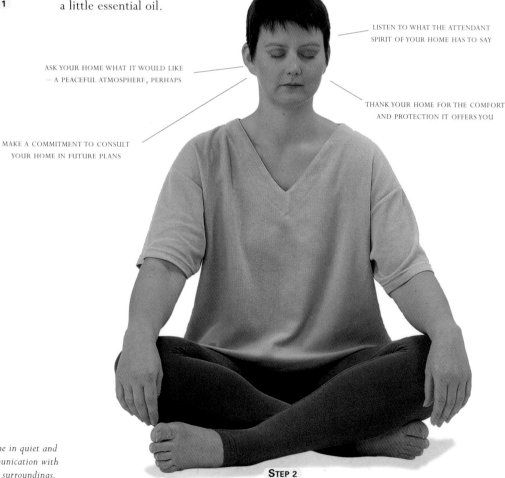

LISTEN TO WHAT THE ATTENDANT
SPIRIT OF YOUR HOME HAS TO SAY

ASK YOUR HOME WHAT IT WOULD LIKE
– A PEACEFUL ATMOSPHERE, PERHAPS

THANK YOUR HOME FOR THE COMFORT
AND PROTECTION IT OFFERS YOU

MAKE A COMMITMENT TO CONSULT
YOUR HOME IN FUTURE PLANS

Spend some time in quiet and reflective communication with your home and surroundings.

STEP 2

ELEMENTS OF THE SOUL HOME

THERE ARE MANY ASPECTS TO THE SOUL HOME. IT NEEDS TO LOOK GOOD AND PLEASE THE EYE, BUT IT ALSO HAS MORE SUBTLE NEEDS. A SOUL HOME HAS AN ATMOSPHERE AND MOOD ALL OF ITS OWN. IT IS THE KIND OF PLACE THAT SHOULD MAKE PEOPLE FEEL INSTANTLY AT HOME. IF YOUR HOME IS A SOUL HOME, PEOPLE WILL LOVE IT INSTINCTIVELY, EVEN IF THEY CANNOT WORK OUT WHY.

SOUL HOMES VERSUS SHOW HOMES

A soul home is certainly not a place of clutter and chaos, but equally it is not a show home. Imbuing your home with soul is not about spending a fortune on new furniture and interior designers: it's about making your home a refuge for the senses, a retreat for the spirit. Some homes make people feel uncomfortable the moment they walk in. The home may look beautiful, but people may not like to sit down in case they crease the cushions. They worry that their children might make a mess or that their dog might dirty the carpet. This kind of home is a statement, like the latest designer clothes or a trendy sports car. A soul home should not be like this. It should be an oasis of refreshment and delight, a feast for the senses.

THE COMFORT ZONE

The appearance of our homes is important, but equally our homes need to *feel* good.

Where possible, choose softly rounded shapes for furnishings, so that the living energy that is present in all things can flow easily around the

Textures and colors should be nurturing.

contours. We also tend to feel more comfortable nestled in a generous sofa with plump cushions than when we are perched on a stiff, square chair. Think about sense-friendly textures too. Given the choice between a luxuriously sensual sheepskin rug and a scratchy synthetic one, which would you rather stretch out on? Choose natural fabrics and furnishings where you can. They connect us with the natural world and make us feel more at home.

Chic surroundings look beautiful but are frequently unwelcoming.

SHIFTING THE MOOD OF YOUR HOME

It is one thing adding texture and comfort to your home, but how do you bring in the right atmosphere and mood? Partly it will come automatically. As you follow the ideas and suggestions in this book, and as you begin to make rituals and blessings part of your daily routine, the atmosphere of your home will naturally change and it will become more creative and fulfilling. But to get you started, try this very simple ritual, versions of which exist in virtually every ancient culture:

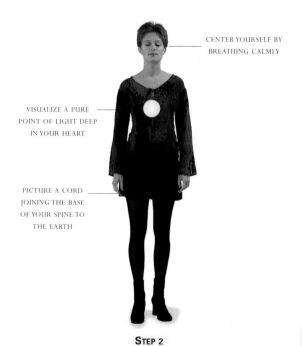

CENTER YOURSELF BY BREATHING CALMLY

VISUALIZE A PURE POINT OF LIGHT DEEP IN YOUR HEART

PICTURE A CORD JOINING THE BASE OF YOUR SPINE TO THE EARTH

STEP 2

1 Stand in the center of your home and take a few moments to ground and center yourself. This is a good technique to use before any visualization exercise: it will enable you to establish an energy connection with the earth, so that you can draw on the earth's energy instead of depleting your own. Ground yourself by visualizing a cord that extends from the base of your spine into the center of the earth. Then center yourself by aligning your body along its center of gravity. Close your eyes and gently follow your breathing. Feel the tension dripping away from your body and mind.

2 Now visualize a small glowing point of light deep in your heart. It shines with a clear, pure, bright, white light.

3 Expand the point of light so it becomes a bubble of light, surrounding your entire body. Know that within this bubble you are safe and protected, serene and secure.

4 Now take the bubble out even farther so that it encompasses the whole of your home, cocooning it in healing, transforming light. Imagine the bubble taking away any negative energy in your home, leaving in its place a pure, beautiful feeling of safety and serenity.

5 Come back to your normal awareness, knowing you have started to transform your home.

VISUALIZE A PROTECTIVE BUBBLE EMBRACING YOU AND YOUR HOME

STEP 3

CLEARING CLUTTER

THE FIRST PRACTICAL STEP YOU CAN TAKE IN TURNING YOUR HOME INTO A REFUGE FOR THE SOUL IS TO CLEAR THE CLUTTER. IT SOUNDS MORE LIKE HOUSEWORK THAN SOULWORK, BUT IT IS ESSENTIAL. THIS DOESN'T MEAN YOU HAVE TO GET RID OF EVERYTHING AND TURN YOUR HOME INTO A TEMPLE OF PURITANICAL MINIMALISM. IT JUST MEANS CLEARING OUT THE UNNECESSARY MESS AND CLUTTER SO THAT YOU CAN FOCUS ON WHAT IS IMPORTANT IN YOUR LIFE.

THE CLUTTER NIGHTMARE

Mess and clutter affect us on three different levels. On a physical level, clutter attracts dust and dirt. A messy house is a nightmare, especially for anyone who suffers from allergies. You can never clean a messy house properly and, since cleanliness is next to soulfulness, this will not help to imbue your home with soul. On a psychological level, clutter makes us feel irritable and tense. Piles of disorganized letters and bills, rooms stuffed with objects, heaps of old newspapers, magazines, and toys all make us feel anxious – our subconscious mind knows there is work to be done and worries about it. On an energy level, clutter is a nightmare. Subtle energy, what the

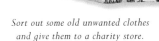

Sort out some old unwanted clothes and give them to a charity store.

Chinese call *ch'i*, cannot flow smoothly and easily where there is clutter. It becomes stuck and turns stagnant, which affects our health and well-being.

HOW TO ELIMINATE CLUTTER

There is no single prescription for clearing clutter. You may want to take it slowly, perhaps clearing a room or just a drawer at a time. Or you may prefer to plunge in and get it all over in one go. Whichever method you choose, there are ways to make the process easier. First it is necessary to look at the various kinds of clutter and how to deal with them.

• CLOTHING: Have you worn it in the last two years? Is it out of fashion? Is it too big or too small? Is it stained or ripped? Does it really suit you? If it isn't something you wear and love, give it to a charity store or rummage sale.

• MAGAZINES AND NEWSPAPERS: Be very organized and cut out any features that

Get rid of those old newspapers.

are of true interest and stick them in a book. Then take the rest to be recycled. Any complete magazines can be donated to hospitals or to your local medical center.

• PAPERWORK: Try to control the amount of paperwork in your home. Put junk mail straight in the trash, or send it back saying you want to be taken off the mailing list; use a reply-paid envelope where possible. Always

cosmetics. Don't throw old medicines in the trash — take them back to your local pharmacy instead so that they can be disposed of safely.

• EXPENSIVE ITEMS: Try selling expensive mistakes and things you no longer like, or give them to someone who couldn't normally afford them.

• NOSTALGIC FAMILY MEMENTOS: These may be ghastly but don't feel guilty — just accept that they are not for you. Is there someone else in the family who might want them? If not, then are they such precious heirlooms? Sell them and have a family dinner on the proceeds.

Clear all the old cosmetics and out-of-date medicines from your bathroom cabinet.

tick the box that asks for your details not to be included on mailing lists. Unless a letter needs a reply or is really useful, put it straight in the trash. Keep an "essential papers" file for vital documents.

• COSMETICS AND MEDICINES: They don't keep forever, so have a purge every year and get rid of any old

TIP

If you find it hard to get rid of mementos, think about what the Chinese sages said: that when you clear away your clutter, you are making room for something new and exciting to come into your life.

SPACE CLEANSING

SPACE CLEANSING IS THE SPIRITUAL EQUIVALENT OF SPRING CLEANING. IT CLEARS YOUR HOME OF UNWANTED PSYCHIC ENERGY. IMAGINE IF YOU HADN'T PHYSICALLY CLEANED YOUR HOME FOR A YEAR — IT WOULD BE FILTHY. MOST OF OUR HOMES HAVE NEVER BEEN CLEANSED ON A SPIRITUAL LEVEL — THEY ARE THE PSYCHIC EQUIVALENT OF RUBBISH DUMPS! THIS CLEANSING RITUAL COMBINES ELEMENTS FROM BALINESE AND NATIVE AMERICAN TRADITIONS.

YOU WILL NEED

- *Rosemary essential oil (optional)*
- *Smudge stick (available from Native American or New Age stores), or lavender essential oil and oil burner*
- *Matches*
- *A large feather to waft the smoke from the smudge stick, if using*
- *Bowl or shell to put the lit smudge stick in, if using*
- *Bell or rattle*

METHOD

1 Take a bath or shower. You might like to add a couple of drops of rosemary oil to the water to help purify your aura. Dress in clean, comfortable clothes, and remove all jewelry and your watch.

2 Go to the center of your home and spend a few moments there with your eyes shut, quietly breathing and centering yourself. You may also be able to contact the spirit of your home and ask for its help (see page 29).

3 Light the smudge stick or oil burner (add seven drops of essential oil to the water reservoir). Call on the spirits of the smudge or lavender to help you purify your space. Use whatever words feel natural.

ESSENTIAL OIL BURNER

You can use a smudge stick or oil burner to refresh the psychic atmosphere of your home. **STEP 3**

Use a feather to waft the fumes around your home.

STEP 4

6 Now go around your home and balance the energy with either a bell or a rattle. To do this, walk around your home again, ringing the bell in each place until you feel you have engaged with the energy there. Imagine you are creating a sacred path of sound that is clearing any last vestiges of old energy.

7 Return to the center of your space and once more close your eyes and breathe. How does you home feel now? Can you detect a difference?

STEP 6

8 Stamp your feet to refresh yourself, shake your body and have a good stretch. It's a good idea to ground yourself after this ritual by having something to eat and drink.

4 Now go around the whole space, using the feather to send smoke or lavender oil fumes into every room and corner of the home.

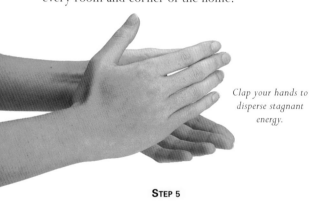

Clap your hands to disperse stagnant energy.

STEP 5

5 Next you will need to "clap out" your home. Move slowly and steadily around your home, and clap out every corner. To do this, clap your hands together, starting at the bottom of the wall and swiftly clapping on up toward the ceiling, as high as you can reach. You may need to repeat this several times in each spot until the sound of your clapping becomes clear. As you clap, visualize your clapping dispersing all the stagnant old energy. When you have finished, wash your hands.

At the end of your cleansing, stamp your feet to refresh yourself.

NOTE

Don't use rosemary essential oil or do space cleansing if you are pregnant. Don't do space cleansing if you are unwell or menstruating.

STEP 8

BRINGING COLOR
TO THE HOME

COLOR HAS BEEN USED FOR THOUSANDS OF YEARS TO ALTER OUR PHYSICAL, EMOTIONAL, AND SPIRITUAL STATES. ACCORDING TO EASTERN PHILOSOPHY, THERE ARE SEVEN GREAT CENTERS OF SUBTLE ENERGY WITHIN OUR BODIES; THESE ARE KNOWN AS THE "CHAKRAS." WE CAN USE THE COLORS OF THE CHAKRAS TO HELP BALANCE OUR BODIES AND SPIRITS, BOTH BY VISUALIZING THEM VIBRATING IN OUR BODIES AND ALSO BY USING THEM THROUGHOUT OUR HOMES.

CHAKRA COLOR AROUND THE HOME

The chakras are visualized as spinning vortices of energy, which are situated in a line down our bodies. Each chakra has its own color vibration starting with deep red at the base of the spine, and then moving through the color spectrum to end with violet at the crown of the head. Think of your home as a body. Just as the chakras in the body move from warm reds and oranges at the bottom to cooler blues, indigos, and violets as they near the head, so the colors in our homes should move from warm reds at the bottom, to cooler shades at the top.

Remember that living a sacred life is not about ignoring the material and physical in favor of lofty ideals and spirituality. Sacred living takes in and honors all aspects of life. So don't feel that a spiritual home needs to be decorated solely in the indigos and violets of the higher chakras. A balanced home will reflect all the chakras and all the colors.

Basically you should think of using the warm, embracing, empowering colors of the lower chakras in the downstairs rooms of your house: living rooms, kitchens, and dining rooms. As you move upstairs to your bedroom, nursery, or study, the colors should become cooler – soft blues and greens are ideal. At the top of your home you might have a meditation room or an attic given over to healing. Here the natural color to choose is the soft violet of deep spirituality.

BALANCING YOUR SOUL WITH COLOR

The colors of the chakras can help you on your path to sacred living. Look around your home and see if there are any colors that are noticeably absent – these could well represent areas of your life that you may find difficult or tend to ignore. Try introducing these "problem" colors into your home, if only in small amounts (maybe a throw, a rug, scatter cushions, or pillows). Be particularly aware if there is a color you really hate – this could be an area of your soul that needs attention.

The main attributes of each chakra and its corresponding color are set out in the chart on the opposite page.

THE CHAKRAS: COLORS AND ATTRIBUTES

BASE CHAKRA: RED	◆ The base chakra is located at the base of the spine. It governs the material world, our physical structure, and our social position in life.
SACRAL CHAKRA: ORANGE	◆ The second chakra is located between the lower abdomen and the navel. It deals with issues of sensuality and sexuality.
SOLAR PLEXUS CHAKRA: YELLOW	◆ The third chakra is found in the solar plexus area. This chakra deals with issues of self-esteem, energy, will, confidence, and inner power.
HEART CHAKRA: GREEN	◆ The fourth chakra is based in the heart and chest. It deals with issues of love, intimacy, emotional balance, and relationships.
THROAT CHAKRA: BLUE	◆ The fifth chakra is located in the throat. It deals with issues of communication and creativity.
BROW CHAKRA: INDIGO	◆ The sixth chakra is situated in the forehead. It deals with imagination, intuition, dreams, and insights.
CROWN CHAKRA: VIOLET	◆ The seventh chakra is found at the crown of the head. It rules understanding and our connection with the Creative Spirit and the divine.

Careful attention to the color balance of your home will help to regulate the flow of energy through it.

BRINGING SOUND INTO YOUR HOME

SOUND HAS THE POWER TO SOOTHE AND CALM, TO ENERGIZE AND UPLIFT. BUT IT ALSO HAS POWER TO HARM, TO IRRITATE OUR NERVES, AND TO MAKE US FEEL TENSE OR DEPRESSED. SO THE SOUNDS YOU CHOOSE FOR YOUR HOME ARE VERY IMPORTANT. SOME PEOPLE MAY LOVE SILENCE OR THE SOUND OF BIRDSONG, OTHERS MAY CRAVE UPBEAT MUSIC AND THE HUM OF LIVELY CONVERSATION. EXPERIMENT TO FIND OUT WHAT YOUR SOUND NEEDS ARE AND HOW TO MEET THEM.

SOUND MEDITATION

This meditation allows you to feel the power of sound reverberating through your body. It helps to balance your chakras (see page 36), and can make you more sensitive to the power of sound.

YOU WILL NEED

◆ *Just yourself*

METHOD

1 Sit comfortably, either on the floor or in a chair. Close your eyes and concentrate on your breathing. Try to take full breaths, so that your abdomen rises as you breathe in, and falls as you breathe out.

2 Start by visualizing your base chakra glowing red in the base of your spine. Make the sound "uh" (like a deep groan), as deep and resonant as

UH

BASE
CHAKRA
(BASE OF
SPINE)

STEP 2

OOOO

GENITAL
CHAKRA

STEP 3

you can. Imagine the sound coming not just from your throat, but also from your base chakra. Keep going as long as feels comfortable – around two minutes is ideal.

3 Now visualize your genital chakra glowing orange, about three inches below the navel. The sound to make for this chakra is "oooo" – still a deep sound but not as profound as "uh." Can you feel this sound resonate in your genital area?

4 The next chakra is in the solar plexus area, between your ribs and navel. Its color is yellow and the sound is a mid-range "oh" (rhyming with "so" and "go").

OH

SOLAR
PLEXUS
CHAKRA

STEP 4

5 Now bring your awareness up into your heart chakra, which glows with a soft, shimmering green. The sound is slightly higher than the solar plexus "oh" – it is a soft and gentle "ah" (as in "father"). Is the sound resonating in your heart? Try to imagine it. Feel your heart expand with love as the "ah" sound vibrates and expands.

STEP 5

HEART CHAKRA
AH

6 Move now to your throat chakra, which shines with a clear, pure blue. The sound here is "eye" as in the word "I." It is higher in tone than the "ah," very clear and almost pellucid. Hear the sound intoning through your throat and vibrating through your body.

EYE
THROAT CHAKRA

STEP 6

THIRD EYE CHAKRA
EY

7 The sixth chakra is located at the site of the "third eye", or spiritual eye, in the center of your forehead. It shines with a pure indigo. Make the sound "ey" (as in "say" or "hay"). The note is higher than the "eye," and very clear and pure. Feel your third eye energized by the sound, and your intuition enlivened. Can you feel the sound in your forehead?

STEP 7

8 The crown chakra located right at the top of your head shimmers with a beautiful purple light. The sound here is the highest of all, a gentle, not shrill, "eee" (as in "me" or "he"). Feel the sound resonating in your crown chakra.

CROWN CHAKRA
EEE

STEP 8

9 Now imagine the crown chakra and your toning linking all the chakras together, so that there is a smooth flow of energy between each of them – a glistening bolt of energy running right through the center of your body.

10 Sit quietly when you have finished and slowly allow yourself to come back to waking consciousness. Stamp your feet to ground yourself – you may need something to eat too.

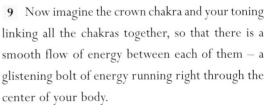

THE BEAUTY OF SCENT IN THE HOME

EVERY ANCIENT CULTURE KNEW THAT SPECIFIC SCENTS HAVE THE POWER TO SHIFT OUR MOODS AND ALTER OUR PERCEPTIONS. NO WONDER INCENSE, SMUDGE STICKS, HERBS, ESSENTIAL OILS, AND RESINS HAVE BEEN USED IN SACRED RITUALS ALL OVER THE WORLD. WE CAN EASILY USE THIS ANCIENT KNOWLEDGE IN OUR OWN QUEST FOR THE SACRED. PLAYING WITH THE SENSE OF SMELL CAN BE A TRULY DELIGHTFUL WAY TO MAKE OURSELVES MORE SENSITIVE AND AWARE.

CHOOSING SCENTS

Choosing scents for your home, and discovering the effects they have on you, can be very enjoyable. This is a matter for the individual – our noses are very refined organs and highly idiosyncratic. You may love the scent of incense or find it totally claustrophobic. Some people adore the scent and smoke of Native American smudge sticks, while others find that the smoke makes them sneeze! It seems as though, at a deeper level, our souls know what we need. Aromatherapists often find that if they allow their patients to pick the oils they most like to smell, they will automatically pick the ones they need for their own healing. So trust your nose and your instincts.

AROMATHERAPY FOR THE SPIRIT

Having said that scents are a matter of individual taste, some aromatherapy oils do seem to affect us in specific ways. The oils shown opposite are universally available and make up an ideal aromatherapy soul-kit for the home.

HOW TO USE ESSENTIAL OILS

There are several ways to use essential oils around the home:
◆ In oil burners – simply add a few drops of essential oil to the water reservoir.
◆ In the bath – add no more than four drops of essential oil to a tablespoon of sweet almond oil or milk, and mix into the bath water.
◆ On a tissue or handkerchief – add a few drops of essential oil and sniff from time to time.
◆ In massage blends – add six drops in total of your chosen oil or oils to 4 teaspoons of sweet almond oil. Mix well.

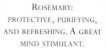

ROSEMARY: PROTECTIVE, PURIFYING, AND REFRESHING. A GREAT MIND STIMULANT.

LAVENDER:
RELAXING, CALMING, CLEANSING, AND PURIFYING. IF YOU CAN ONLY BUY ONE OIL, MAKE IT LAVENDER.

CAUTION

Always choose the best quality, purest oils you can find. Only use in the amounts specified — aromatherapy is potent medicine and can be harmful if used incorrectly. Certain oils should not be used for children, for pregnant women, or for those who have a serious medical condition — always check with a qualified aromatherapist.

LEMON:
STIMULATING, REFRESHING, CHEERING, AND CLEANSING; EASES STRESS.

BERGAMOT:
REFRESHING AND UPLIFTING; SOOTHES THE PAIN OF GRIEF; EASES ANXIETY, DEPRESSION, AND STRESS.

SANDALWOOD:
RELAXING, PURIFYING, UPLIFTING, BALANCING, AND APHRODISIAC; HELPS CUT EMOTIONAL TIES.

YLANG YLANG:
CALMING, SOOTHING, CHEERING, AND APHRODISIAC; PUTS YOU IN TOUCH WITH YOUR SENSUALITY.

GERANIUM:
CHEERING AND UPLIFTING; IDEAL FOR PARTIES.

MANDARIN:
UPLIFTING, CHEERING, BALANCING, AND REVITALIZING; CAN EASE DEPRESSION AND INSOMNIA.

JUNIPER:
DEEPLY PURIFYING, CLEANSING, AND PROTECTIVE; CLEARS AND FOCUSES THE MIND.

ATTRACTING THE ELEMENTS

ESOTERIC PHILOSOPHY TEACHES THAT THE WORLD IS COMPOSED OF FIVE ELEMENTS: EARTH, FIRE, WATER, AIR, AND SPIRIT. GETTING IN TOUCH WITH EACH OF THESE VITAL ELEMENTS CAN HELP US CONNECT WITH THE SACRED. ALL GOOD RITUALS INCLUDE THESE ELEMENTS, EITHER FOCUSING ON ONE OR TWO, OR INCORPORATING THEM ALL. START BY THINKING ABOUT HOW YOU CAN BRING THE ELEMENTAL FORCES INTO YOUR HOME.

HOW TO BRING IN THE ELEMENTS

There are many simple ways to attract the power of four of the elements – earth, fire, water, and air – into your home. It is not necessary to try to attract the fifth element, spirit, because it is the pure essence of spirit that you will automatically invoke when you perform rituals or try to live in a sacred way. Here are suggestions for bringing the other four elements into your home:

EARTH

Earth grounds us; it gives us safety, stability, and a center. It often represents the physical level, our bodies, and the earth itself.
♦ The most obvious way of bringing the earth element into your home is with natural stone and rock, or ceramics and earthenware.
♦ Sea salt represents earth; use it in your rituals.
♦ Crystals are powerful stores of earth energy. Go to a crystal store and let your intuition pick one.

AIR

Air is invigorating, fresh, and incisive. It is usually associated with the intellect, the sharp power of the mind.
♦ Burn incense, smudge sticks, and aromatherapy oils to attract the spirits of the air; they can also be used in rituals.
♦ Open your windows once or twice a day and let the fresh breeze blow through your home.

WATER

Water soothes, calms, purifies, and heals. It represents our emotions.
♦ Bowls of water, perhaps with floating candles or flower petals, look attractive and give valuable humidity.
♦ Introduce water into rituals by spraying the room with a plant mister. You can add aromatherapy oils or flower remedies (available from health stores) of your own choice to intensify the effect.
♦ Install an interior waterfall – it is very soothing.

FIRE

Fire is pure energy. It ushers in new possibilities and has protective qualities. It usually represents the will, and the energy of the heart.
♦ Candles can be used both in rituals and to energize your home, but make sure they are positioned in a safe place.
♦ An open fire is warming and comforting. It is also a wonderful place to meditate and dream.

SIMPLE FIRE RITUAL
FOR THE HOME

YOU WILL NEED

- *Sheet of paper and a pen*
- *An open fire, or a candle and flameproof bowl*

CAUTION

If using the candle method, for safety purposes be sure to have a flameproof bowl handy. Put the paper into the bowl as soon as it begins to burn.

Write what you wish for your home on a piece of paper and offer it to the fire spirits.

METHOD

1 Write down on a piece of paper all that you desire for your home. If you prefer, you can draw or paint a picture instead.

2 Now dedicate the paper to the power of the fire spirits, asking them to take your wishes and help you make them happen.

3 Put the paper into the flames of a fire or over a lit candle and watch it burn. Imagine the fire taking your dreams and turning them into reality.

FLAMEPROOF BOWL

CHAPTER THREE

SACRED AREAS
IN THE HOME

FOR THOUSANDS OF YEARS PEOPLE HAVE BUILT ALTARS AND SHRINES. THEY HAVE
DEDICATED CERTAIN PLACES TO THE SACRED AND USED THEM AS PLACES OF PRAYER,
MEDITATION, RITUAL, AND RENEWAL. ARCHEOLOGISTS HAVE FOUND EVIDENCE OF
PRIMITIVE ALTARS, SACRED OBJECTS, AND FIGURINES ALL OVER THE WORLD, FROM
ANATOLIA TO BALI, FROM CHINA TO SCANDINAVIA. IT SEEMS AS THOUGH BUILDING
ALTARS IS A VERY DEEP-SEATED HUMAN URGE.

NATURAL ALTARS

Altars have taken many shapes and forms. The first were probably the natural sacred spaces: places that seemed to our ancestors to be heavily imbued with the sacred, perhaps the dwelling place of a god, goddess, or nature spirit. Mountain tops, caves, springs, and groves were freely venerated. Offerings would be left and over time the place would become a natural shrine. As humans learned more sophisticated building techniques, they used their architecture to create temples, churches, and mosques as a home for the spirit.

AN UNBROKEN TRADITION

Throughout history the simpler tradition of home altars and shrines has also remained. Humans have always strived to bring the divine into their homes, to imbue everyday life with a sense of the sacred. Many religious traditions have continued the practice unbroken to the present day: step into any orthodox Hindu or Catholic home and you will usually find a shrine. Images of Buddha and Kuan-yin will adorn the homes of Buddhists or Taoists. For Native Americans the Medicine Wheel is a gateway to the spirit, while most modern Wiccans or followers of other nature-based Earth religions will have one or more altars with images of the Goddess and nature in their homes.

WHY BUILD AN ALTAR?

Personal altars offer us the chance to make the divine personal. An altar should always reflect our own personality, beliefs, and needs – everything you place on your altar should have meaning. Then, whenever you see your altar, you will become mindful of the sacred in your life. An altar is a small place of refuge, an aid to stilling the mind. You can also make altars for specific purposes, so if you want to bring more success, or love, or peace into your life, you could construct an altar for that purpose.

HOW WE MAKE
SUBCONSCIOUS ALTARS

MOST LIKELY, IF YOU LOOK AROUND YOUR HOME, YOU MAY ALREADY HAVE MADE ONE OR MORE ALTARS WITHOUT REALIZING IT. AS WE HAVE SEEN, IT IS A HUMAN NEED TO FIND MEANING AND THE SACRED IN PARTICULAR PLACES AND WITH CERTAIN GROUPINGS OF OBJECTS. A SHELF, A TABLE, OR EVEN A MANTELPIECE MAY ALREADY BE FULFILLING SOME OF THE FUNCTIONS OF AN ALTAR IN YOUR OWN HOME WITHOUT YOUR BEING AWARE OF IT.

Look around your home. Do you have a particular table where you keep photographs of your family, favorite souvenirs, and cherished heirlooms? You may not realize it, but you have subconsciously made a family altar, celebrating your family past and present. A dressing table might be another place where you automatically group objects that have intrinsic beauty and meaning for you. Or is there a shelf or window sill somewhere where a statue of a god or goddess sits next to a candle or an aromatherapy burner?

A child's special arrangement of soft toys creates a sacred space.

EVERYDAY SHRINES

Any area of the home can be a natural altar. We decorate our refrigerator doors with photographs and mementos, postcards from dear friends, and inspirational images.

A table with a family photograph makes a beautiful altar.

Our bedside table often contains our most personal or cherished possessions: a journal or diary, a book of sacred sayings, a photo of our nearest and dearest, maybe a night-light, a crystal, or a beautiful ornament. These are the things that soothe us into peaceful sleep. Likewise, a child will automatically arrange her toys in very precise order. She may not settle unless teddy, her favorite dolls, and soft toys are all in their correct places. She is naturally creating sacred order.

DESK SHRINES

Virtually everyone who works at a desk turns it, to some degree, into an altar, and many people who work with computers decorate them in some way. Given the power of altars to bring different energies into your life, it is advisable to plan your desk with precision for well-being and success. The ideas given here include tips from *Feng Shui*, the ancient Chinese art of placement (see also pages 60–63).

• Keep your desk as clear and uncluttered as possible.

• Put a picture of your partner or family on the far right corner of your desk to ensure good relationships.

• Have something red or golden on the far left corner of your desk – a healthy plant in a bright red pot is ideal – and it will help to boost finances. Keep this area well lit.

• Reference books should be well to your left – the area of inner knowledge.

• Your address book should be on your right, in the area of helpful people.

• Straight in front of you, or on your computer, have something inspirational: a deity, crystal, stone, flowers, or picture that symbolizes what you want from your work.

• Have a candle burning, to keep your energy high.

• An essential oil burner is ideal – use rosemary and juniper to aid concentration, lavender or geranium to keep you calm and centered.

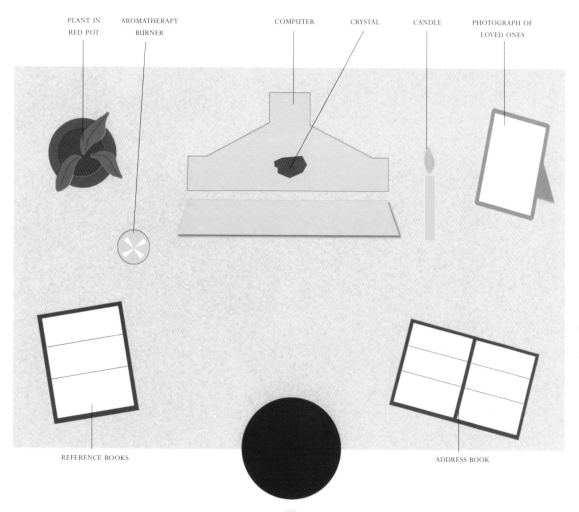

PLANT IN RED POT   AROMATHERAPY BURNER   COMPUTER   CRYSTAL   CANDLE   PHOTOGRAPH OF LOVED ONES

REFERENCE BOOKS   ADDRESS BOOK

FINDING SACRED
SPACE IN THE HOME

HOW DO WE FIND SACRED SPACE IN OUR HOMES? HOW CAN WE TELL WHERE TO PUT AN ALTAR OR SHRINE? AS WE HAVE SEEN, THERE MAY ALREADY BE PARTICULAR PLACES IN YOUR HOME THAT YOU HAVE IMBUED WITH A SENSE OF SOMETHING SPECIAL OR SPIRITUAL. IF SO, THESE PLACES COULD WELL BE THE NATURALLY SACRED AREAS THAT YOU ARE SEEKING, BUT THERE ARE OTHER POTENTIALLY SACRED AREAS OF YOUR HOME THAT ARE EASY TO OVERLOOK.

YOUR HOME ALTAR

Every home usually has a key area that holds the spirit of the house and offers refuge and a home for the sacred. You may automatically know where it should be – maybe there is already a form of subconscious altar there. If not, try this simple exercise. Close your eyes, center yourself, and breathe calmly. Ask for guidance on where to place your altar: ask your higher Self, your guardians, and the spirit of your home. Most likely you will find that you suddenly get a strong feeling or a vague sense of where your home altar should be.

OTHER ALTARS

You can build altars all over your home. Many ancient cultures have some kind of shrine or sanctuary on or around the threshold of the house that offers protection and signals the shift from the outside world to the sacred home. A kitchen is a natural place for a homey altar where you can offer thanks for all your blessings. A living room could prove home to a family or friends altar, celebrating love and warmth. More private altars can be sited

in your bedroom, study, or meditation space. Even small spaces, such as a window ledge, the top of a cupboard, or even a series of hanging baskets in your bathroom, can make effective homes for altars.

A SPACE OF YOUR OWN

If at all possible, you should try to find a space you can truly call your own to use for meditation, a ritual, or simply as a place in which you can sit quietly and refresh your soul. If you have the space, a whole room given over to the sacred is a wonderful gift to your soul. Decorate and furnish it as your spirit dictates. It could be as pure and clear as a

Natural elements can bring the divine into your home.

monastic cell, or buzzing with energy and full of color, art, and sacred objects. If you do not have the gift of a room of your own, find other places in the home that can become permanent havens. There could be a corner of the kitchen, perhaps with a rocking chair by the fire. It might be as simple as a particular window sill that just has "that" feeling. Trust your intuition and find the places that call to your soul. Make them special by using them for your rituals. Enliven them with a vase of flowers, a candle, a gift from nature. Or use the bubble meditation (see pages 30–31) to set a psychic magic circle around your spaces. Claim them for your own.

Many Eastern cultures value domestic shrines.

The light of a candle symbolizes warmth and life.

DEDICATING YOUR SPACE

Different cultures have various ceremonies to dedicate an altar or a space to the sacred, but all you really need is intent. This ritual focuses your will and spiritual intent, and calls on the power of the elements — an idea common to many sacred traditions. Always perform this ritual before using a space for an altar or for ritual purposes — it clears the psychic atmosphere and leaves it clear for your own chosen vibrations.

YOU WILL NEED

- *Juniper or rosemary essential oil (optional)*
- *Incense, or juniper essential oil and burner, or a smudge stick with a bowl and large feather (see page 34)*
- *Matches*
- *Bowl of water*
- *Bowl of sea salt*
- *Candle*
- *A cleansed crystal (see step 7, opposite), optional*

The cleansing fumes of essential oils or incense will purify the atmosphere around your shrine.

METHOD

1 Make sure your space has been thoroughly cleaned. You could add a few drops of juniper or rosemary essential oil to your cleaning water or polish to add protective qualities.

2 Gather all your materials in the chosen space or in front of the altar area you wish to dedicate.

STEP 3

3 Light the incense, oil, or smudge stick. This represents the element of air. Waft the scented smoke around the space, asking the Spirit of Air to help you cleanse the area.

STEP 4

4 Place the bowl of water in the center of the chosen space. Hold your hands over it and ask the Spirit of Water to help you with your dedication. Imagine your intention for this space pouring into the water, blending with the soothing, healing power of water. Scoop some water in your hand and flick it into each corner of the space, sending your love and intent with it.

STEP 5

5 Now take the bowl of salt, which represents the Spirit of Earth. Feel your feet firmly on the floor – imagine yourself rooted to the earth below. Ask the great Spirit of Earth to keep this space grounded and protected. Sprinkle a little salt in a thin line around your space.

6 Finally, light the candle, which represents the Spirit of Fire. Quietly watch the flame flickering and burning. Appreciate its life and energy. Ask the Spirit of Fire to energize and inspire your space, and to imbue it with its fiercely protective and transformative power.

STEP 6

7 If you wish, you could also dedicate a crystal to help boost the sacred power of your space. Only use the crystal after it has been cleansed. To do this, put it in a bowl of salt water for at least 36 hours, then dry it carefully.

Energize a crystal to boost the power of your sacred space.

8 Take the newly cleansed crystal and hold it to your heart. Imagine your heart chakra pulsing with energy and your sacred intent for the space. Now send that energy into the crystal, charging it to keep the energy of that place secure. Put the crystal on your altar or special place.

9 Finish by visualizing your space surrounded by bright, white, pure light. Say a prayer if you wish, and thank the spirits who have helped you in this ritual.

MAKING AN ALTAR

How do you make an altar? There are really no set rules. You should follow your intuition and be guided by what feels right. However, if you feel uncertain, there are various tried and tested formulas that will start you on the right track. Here are some suggestions for building a basic home altar.

YOU WILL NEED

- Candles (see the Candle Chart, opposite)
- Bowl of water
- Incense and incense holder, or essential oil and oil burner
- Matches
- Bowl of salt

Optional:

- A healthy plant or vase of fresh flowers
- Favorite photos
- Cleansed crystals (see page 51)
- Representations of divinities
- Natural objects, such as stones, wood, and shells
- Other meaningful objects

METHOD

1 First dedicate your altar (see pages 50–51).

2 The candles, water, incense, and salt symbolize the four elements of fire, water, air, and earth, which traditionally are represented on any altar for balance and connection. Position them as you wish. You may like to add flowers or petals to the water in the bowl. Choose an incense or essential oil that you like or that suits your purpose for your altar (see pages 40–41). The color of the candle you choose may also reflect your purpose (see the Candle Chart, opposite).

Gather together natural objects to decorate your altar.

3 Now you can add more items to personalize your altar if you wish. If you are building a home altar, you may like to include more flowers, and pictures of your family, or items made by them. Things that represent your common or various interests can be included too. If you have a preferred deity, it is good to include an image or symbol: this may be a figure of Buddha or the Goddess, a cross, or a Star of David.

4 Feel free to play around with the arrangement until it feels right. Light the candle and let your mind wander over the altar. Does it have a good atmosphere? Does it inspire you, or provide a focus for meditation? Does it set your mind on interesting pathways? If so, the altar is doing its job.

CANDLE CHART

There are many varying associations for different candle colors, but the following work well:

 BLUE
♦ For meditation, or for bedroom altars where you want a relaxing and soothing atmosphere.

 PURPLE
♦ For psychic development and spiritual awareness. Purple works well for a private meditation altar.

 GREEN
♦ For a healing altar, and to bring balance, peace, and harmony. Green also attracts wealth and abundance.

 YELLOW
♦ For friendship and joy. Use for increased communication, good luck, wisdom, exams, and for a home office altar.

 RED
♦ For passion and energy. Red is a powerful color for attracting romance and sex.

 PINK
♦ Ideal if you are seeking love, or if you want to conceive a child.

The altar that you create will reflect your own personality. There are no rules: simply follow the promptings of your inmost self.

ALTARS FOR EVERY PURPOSE

ONCE YOU HAVE GRASPED THE BASIC PRINCIPLES OF ALTAR BUILDING, YOU WILL FIND IT SIMPLE TO CREATE ALTARS FOR ANY ROOM OR FOR ANY PURPOSE. JUST BEAR IN MIND THAT YOU ARE PROVIDING A VISUAL FOCUS FOR YOUR INTENT, SO INCLUDE ITEMS THAT HAVE A PARTICULARLY STRONG MEANING AND RESONANCE FOR YOU. IT HELPS IF YOU TRY TO PERSONALIZE YOUR ALTARS AS MUCH AS POSSIBLE. HERE ARE SOME MORE IDEAS FOR DIFFERENT KINDS OF ALTARS.

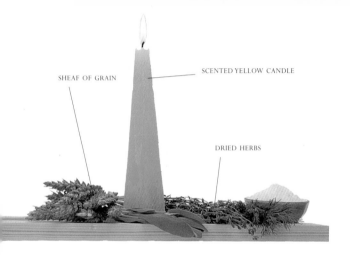

SHEAF OF GRAIN   SCENTED YELLOW CANDLE

DRIED HERBS

A KITCHEN ALTAR

This altar could find a home on top of the refrigerator, on the mantelpiece of the fire, or on a kitchen shelf.

• The goddess of the kitchen and the bounty of the harvest is Demeter, so honor her with a sheaf of grain or a grain dolly.

• Add a yellow candle to bring friendship and warmth to the kitchen, and keep it burning all through the day if possible. Put the candle in a bowl of water or sand for safety.

• Keep a bowl of salt on the altar, and some bundles of dried herbs: sage symbolizes wisdom, thyme is purifying, dill brings prosperity, and fennel helps your household spirits to guard against negativity.

• Add a vase of flowers or fresh herbs.

AN ALTAR FOR A CHILD'S ROOM

This simple altar could be placed on a window ledge, above a crib or bed, or on a shelf in a nursery or child's room. If your child is small, make sure the altar is well out of reach.

• Add an image of one of the protective mother goddesses: the Virgin Mary, Isis, Demeter, Kuan-yin, or other mother deity should take center stage.

• If your child has a protective animal guide, or is fond of an animal, add a soft toy or picture of it.

- Pink or white night-lights can be added, but make sure they are in safe containers, or in bowls of water or sand.
- Rose quartz makes a lovely guardian crystal for a child. Cleanse it first (see pages 50–51).
- Add a photo of your child surrounded by pictures of important, caring people such as parents, grandparents, and godparents.
- Dried garlic is very protective – sew a small pouch and put the garlic in it, then add some lavender.

A HEALING BATHROOM ALTAR

You may not feel you have a lot of space in your bathroom but, if you don't have a spare shelf, buy a hanging bath-tidy that contains three or four metal baskets. Hang it over your bathtub or shower so that it receives the steam but not direct water.

ESSENTIAL OIL BURNER

BAG OF PURIFYING HERBS

WATER-LOVING PLANTS

Altars for the bathroom can be suspended from the ceiling.

A child's altar should include symbols of protection: teddies, guardian statues, and a family photograph.

- The bottom basket could contain a healthy green plant that thrives in humid atmospheres – ferns do very well.
- Make a bag of healing, purifying herbs and hang it from a basket or place it inside – include thyme, mint, rosemary, lemon balm, and lavender. The steam will release their healing vapors.
- Celebrate nature by using one basket to house a collection of beautiful colored stones and shells, and pieces of driftwood.
- Put an essential oil burner at the top; soothing oils include lavender, sandalwood, and chamomile. Add a candle – blue is good for a peaceful, relaxing bath.

CHAPTER FOUR

MEALTIME RITUALS

FOOD HAS ALWAYS BEEN LINKED WITH THE SACRED. IT IS ONLY IN RECENT YEARS THAT WE HAVE LOST OUR SACRED CONNECTION WITH THE FOOD THAT SUSTAINS US. NOWADAYS MANY OF US BARELY NOTICE WHAT WE EAT: WE EAT ON THE RUN, OR GULP DOWN "FAST FOOD." FEW OF US SIT DOWN AS A FAMILY TO ENJOY NUTRITIOUS, LOVINGLY PREPARED FOOD. THIS CHAPTER WILL FOCUS ON HOW WE CAN ENJOY FOOD AS SPIRITUAL AS WELL AS PHYSICAL SUSTENANCE.

RELIGION AND FOOD

All the great religions teach that food is a blessing from the divine and should be treated with respect and gratitude. No Jewish, Christian, Hindu, Muslim, or Buddhist family would dream of starting a meal without first saying a blessing and giving thanks. In China, food is considered to be a physical link between humans and the gods; beautifully prepared meals are given as sacred offerings on family altars. In the Ayurvedic tradition of India, food is a spiritual science, with precise prescriptions of how to prepare and eat food for physical, emotional, and spiritual well-being

Although the rituals and customs may vary, all these traditions have several things in common. First, they recognize that food is far more than mere fuel for the body; it also sustains the soul. Second, they believe in the mindful planning, preparation, and consumption of food. Third, they insist on the necessity to give thanks for the food they eat. Most of them also sanctify the ritual of eating together with their loved ones.

SOUL FOOD

In African-American culture there is the tradition of "soul food." Soul food is food that is cooked with love, intent, intuition, and a sense of history. It is a living prayer and celebration, and has much to teach us. At first it may seem crazy to think that how we prepare our food can have an effect on us. And yet the latest research indicates that this might be exactly what happens. Nutritionists and psychologists have, for many years, been discovering that the food we eat can have specific effects on our psychological state. They have dubbed the feel-good foods "mood foods." But now these experts are amazed to find that how the food is prepared can actually affect our spiritual state and well-being.

Food freshly prepared, and cooked lovingly by hand, has more vital energy than processed, factory prepared food. Some experiments have even shown that "healing" the food, in other words imbuing it with love while we prepare it, can make it taste better! So when you cook with love and eat with attention, you are taking in the very stuff of life.

HOW TO MAKE
MEALTIMES SPECIAL

YOU DO NOT NEED TO SPEND INORDINATE AMOUNTS OF TIME AND MONEY TO MAKE MEALTIMES INTO A CELEBRATION OF SOUL FOOD. THE SIMPLEST OF RITUALS CAN TURN EVEN A HUMBLE SANDWICH INTO A FEAST FOR THE SPIRIT. THE PRINCIPLES OF MAKING MEALTIMES SACRED ARE VERY STRAIGHTFORWARD, AND THEY CAN EASILY BE ADAPTED TO FIT YOUR CIRCUMSTANCES AND PREFERENCES. JUST REMEMBER TO PREPARE YOUR FOOD WITH LOVE, AND IT WILL NOURISH AND SUSTAIN YOU.

HOW TO PREPARE A SOUL MEAL

Preparing soul food need not involve new recipes or expensive ingredients. Just follow these simple principles to transform the food you eat.

• Take care when choosing your food: pick the freshest, most local, seasonal, organic food you can find. If you eat meat, ensure it has been farmed with care and consideration for the animals. Think about growing for yourself some of the things you eat, even if it's just a selection of herbs in a window box.

Fresh, simple ingredients are all you need.

• Say a prayer or blessing before you start. Hold your hands over the ingredients and thank them for giving their life for you. Visualize the journey of those ingredients: how they grew, who tended them, and how they came to be on your table. Ask them to nourish you and your family with love.

• Prepare your food with love and attention. Concentrate on the task at hand – look on it as sacred meditation. Try not to distract yourself by watching television or listening to the radio as you cook. Take time to notice the textures, scents, and feel of the food you are cooking. Avoid gadgets and food processors wherever possible – chopping by hand brings you into closer contact with the food.

Visualize your food in its natural state.

58

• Think of your cooking as sacred alchemy. Remember you are using all the elements in your cooking: the earth of your raw ingredients; water to cook in; as you stir or beat you are adding in air; and last there is the fire of your stove.

• As you cook, pour in your hopes and wishes for the people who will eat your food. Focus your intention as you chop, stir, mix, and blend. Think of cooking as a kind of spell-making. Add herbs and spices with a view to their magical properties as well as their healing ones, and you can increase the power. For example, use rosemary for protection and courage, dill for prosperity, and sage for wisdom.

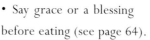

Enliven your cooking space with fresh flowers.

• Say grace or a blessing before eating (see page 64).

• Eat your food mindfully. Smell the different fragrances before you start to eat. Notice how you choose your food and be aware of putting it on your fork and in your mouth. Don't just swallow it – really taste the food and feel its texture. Make each mouthful a mindful one.

• Allow time in your meal for conversation and a sense of community. Don't race to get up from the table afterward – sit and talk instead. Relax and enjoy the company.

• Clean up with mindfulness and gratitude. Try adding a few drops of mandarin oil to your dish washing liquid to cheer your senses.

Prepare the meal by hand so as to be in close harmony with the food.

• Lay your table with care. Even the simplest meals can be made special by adding a small vase of flowers (a posy of wild flowers, buds, or leaves is inexpensive and will look lovely); you could also add a candle. There are more ideas for table decoration in the pages that follow.

• Serve your meal so that it looks as inviting and appetizing as possible. Choose foods in colors that complement each other.

Clearing up after the meal is an opportunity to recall the joyful experience that you have just shared.

FENG SHUI FOR HARMONIOUS MEALTIMES

The ancient Chinese art of Feng Shui can be useful when you're seeking harmonious mealtimes. How you place your guests around the table can make all the difference between a dinner party success and a failure. If your family gatherings regularly turn into brawls, a little Feng Shui will transform a Sunday dinner into a pleasant, warm occasion. It can even help bring people together and keep warring factions at peace.

FAMILY MEALS

This table setting should make a large family gathering run smoothly.

• Lay the table with care. The tablecloth and napkins should be in warm earth colors – gold, beige, and warm brown – to increase acceptance. These colors also encourage those who are shy and unsociable, and anchor those who are fiery.

• If there is a lot of tension within your family, make sure you have a soft, gentle flower arrangement in the middle of the table to help calm everyone down.

Family mealtimes can be an enriching experience for all involved.

Arrange your flowers in a glass bowl so that the water is clearly visible.

• The head and foot of the table are the two key positions, so in a standard two-parent family, the parents should sit at either end. Chinese philosophy also honors grandparents, so if you have older relatives at your table, they should hold court at one end of the table.

• If you have a difficult or irascible child or other family member, he or she will tend be more restrained if placed next to the mother or father, or older relatives.

• Difficult people can be soothed by playing gentle classical music or something happy and loving that they will like.

• Dim the lights to lower the energy – this can be helpful if the situation is likely to be volatile.

TIPS FOR PERFECT DINING

• Tables should ideally be wooden, with gently rounded shapes for harmony.

• Incorporate all the Chinese elements on your table: a decanter of wine or water represents water;

cutlery or metal ornaments represent metal; candles or an overhead light symbolize fire; the table and any plants or flower arrangements represent wood; and ceramics and earthenware, glasses (which are made from sand), and decorative arrangements of stones or rocks symbolize earth.

• The colors you choose for your tablecloth and napkins are very important and should be selected with care: greens and blues are cool tones that tend to reduce our appetites – you might use them for light afternoon meals; reds and oranges are often used in restaurants and cafés because they stimulate appetite and create a lively, energetic atmosphere; golds and pinks are good for friendship and tend to create a happy, convivial atmosphere; yellows and browns are harmonious colors and help to create a calm, contented atmosphere.

• Keep the doors in your dining room shut while you are eating, otherwise the flow of energy can make you feel anxious and hurried.

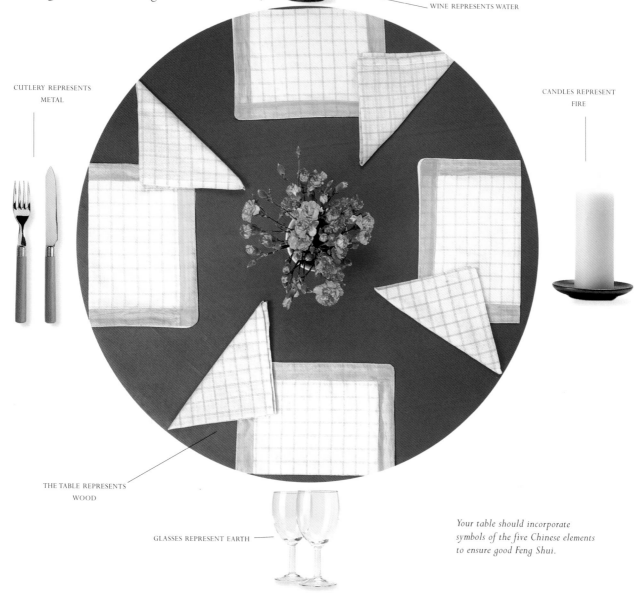

WINE REPRESENTS WATER

CUTLERY REPRESENTS METAL

CANDLES REPRESENT FIRE

THE TABLE REPRESENTS WOOD

GLASSES REPRESENT EARTH

Your table should incorporate symbols of the five Chinese elements to ensure good Feng Shui.

FENG SHUI FOR DIFFERENT OCCASIONS

Whether you are planning a romantic dinner for two or an important business meeting, the Chinese art of Feng Shui can help you achieve the outcome you desire. By setting the table in a particular way, choosing shapes and colors that attract the right energy, and positioning yourself and your guests in the appropriate places, you allow positive forces to flow smoothly and beneficially on your behalf.

A ROMANTIC DINNER

This table setting can promote a feeling of intimacy and warmth.

• Choose a round table and cover it with a purple, lilac, or mauve tablecloth. The table shouldn't be too large – it needs to feel intimate.

• You should be seated at right angles to your partner so that you can talk easily.

• Candlelight may sound like a cliché, but it is essential. Choose just one candlestick. The candle should be no more than two or three inches high so that it does not create a barrier between you. You might like to set it on a small, polished mirror to draw you closer together.

• A vase of flowers should be placed on the other side of the table so that it doesn't come between you.

• A champagne bucket (with champagne!) will also help the mood.

SIT AT RIGHT ANGLES TO YOUR PARTNER

Good Feng Shui will enhance the sense of intimacy.

KEEP THE FLOWERS TO THE SIDE – SO THEY DON'T COME BETWEEN YOU

A BUSINESS LUNCH

If you are meeting important clients, it is essential that you feel as comfortable as possible and exude a sense of calm confidence. Try this table setting.

HOLD THE KEY POSITION. MAKE SURE YOU HAVE FULL VIEW OF THE DOOR AND ARE DIRECTLY OPPOSITE YOUR GUEST

JUNIOR STAFF MEMBERS SHOULD BE SEATED AT YOUR LEFT

PLACE YOUR GUEST DIRECTLY OPPOSITE YOU

• Choose for yourself a chair with a back that is reasonably close to a wall. You should be in the power position – diagonally opposite the door.

• Invite the more senior of your guests to sit opposite you. This will please them because, sitting opposite, they will have direct contact with you. A more junior person should sit on your left, which is good for harmonious discussions.

• If possible, choose a round table – it will help to ensure that energy flows smoothly and business talks run profitably.

Business success and prosperity will be assured if you pay attention to the principles of Feng Shui when organizing meetings with clients.

• A round glass or a paperweight makes a good centerpiece, perhaps arranged with flowers or candles. Put three coins under the glass paperweight and a mirror under the coins. The three coins represent growth and movement connected to money, and the glass paperweight strengthens the intuition of all concerned and will help to create a harmonious settlement.

BLESSINGS AND GRACES

EVERY RELIGION HAS ITS OWN VARIETIES OF BLESSINGS AND GRACES. NOWADAYS MOST OF US RARELY SAY GRACE, UNLESS WE HAPPEN TO BE AT A LARGE FORMAL OCCASION. YET SAYING GRACE GIVES US THE CHANCE TO THINK ABOUT THE BLESSINGS WE ENJOY. WHILE WE ARE TRYING TO LIVE OUR LIVES IN AN INSPIRED AND SACRED WAY, LET'S TAKE THE OPPORTUNITY OF BRINGING THIS SMALL BUT IMPORTANT RITUAL BACK INTO EVERYDAY USE.

A BLESSING BASED ON JEWISH TRADITION

This is a much simplified and adapted version of a traditional Jewish ceremony. The elements are also similar to Christian and Pagan ceremonies.

STEP 1

1   Before you eat, light several small candles and place them around the table. Ask each person to say a few words of thanks, expressing their pleasure at being together to share a meal.

2   Now pick up a glass of wine and
STEP 2   hold it aloft. The glass or cup represents

holiness and the link between God and humankind. Say a prayer of thanks for the blessings you have been given. Share the wine and let everyone take a sip.

3   Now pick up a loaf of bread and think about the incredible process that brought the bread to your table. It started with a tiny seed that grew under the sun, nourished by the earth. It was harvested, threshed, milled into flour, and then kneaded and baked into bread to feed you. Give everyone a piece of bread and invite them to give thanks in their own way for this gift of life.

4   Now you can all start to eat your meal together, with mindfulness and pleasure.

Bread is one of the most basic gifts of nature.

An acknowledgment of the work that produced our food enriches our enjoyment.

The sharing of food is a central part of belonging to a community.

MUSLIM SACREDNESS AT MEALTIMES

In Islam, food is considered to be sacred, and Muslims are expected to approach mealtimes with a deep sense of gratitude for the goodness and bounty of Allah. They have several customs that can help us bring sacredness to our tables.

• It is traditional to be hospitable and welcoming to guests. Make some of your mealtimes special by inviting extended family, friends, or neighbors to eat with you. Social duty is held in esteem, so perhaps think of someone needy who might appreciate an invitation. It maybe an elderly neighbor or someone who is new to the area.

• Muslims often serve food in one large dish or on an immense platter. Everyone takes food from the same pot, choosing the portion of food that is closest to them. This symbolizes the sharing, caring aspect of the family or group and is a good way of drawing people together.

• Before you eat, take a few moments for everyone to say their own silent prayers of thanks and appreciation. Silent grace is a lovely idea because it removes the need for what can become formulaic set graces and gives each person the chance to say what he or she wishes.

SOUL PAMPERING SUPPER

WHETHER WE LIVE ALONE OR JUST HAVE THE OCCASIONAL EVENING ON OUR OWN, MOST OF US FIND OURSELVES EATING ALONE FROM TIME TO TIME. OFTEN WE DON'T MAKE AN EFFORT FOR OURSELVES, SO THIS RITUAL, LOOSELY BASED ON GREEK MYTHOLOGY, CAN MAKE A WELCOME CHANGE. IT BOOSTS OUR SELF-ESTEEM AS WELL AS LETTING US REMEMBER THAT WE CAN HONOR SACRED MEALTIMES AS MUCH ON OUR OWN AS WITH OTHER PEOPLE.

YOU WILL NEED

- 6 pink candles
- 6 drops mandarin or sweet orange essential oil
- A selection of your favorite foods
- Bowl of fresh flowers
- Fresh sprigs of rosemary or lavender
- Pen and paper

METHOD

1 Start by having a long relaxing soak in a bath. Light pink candles around the bathtub and add the uplifting mandarin or orange oil to the bathwater, and disperse well. Lie in the bath and spend some time appreciating your body. You may like to imagine you are Aphrodite in her pool, surrounded by nymphs who tend to your every whim. Enjoy their compliments.

2 Dry yourself and dress in comfortable, clean clothes. Pure cotton or silk is ideal. Enjoy the feeling of the cloth on your clean skin.

3 Prepare the table for your supper with care and attention. Place a beautiful piece of cloth on the table — you might try a length of sari fabric or a large silk scarf. Rearrange the pink candles around the room and on the table, and put some fresh flowers in a bowl or vase. You might like to sprinkle petals on the table or strew sweet-smelling herbs such as lemon verbena, woodruff, and borage. Wind some rosemary or lavender into a napkin ring.

A meal alone is an opportunity to honor yourself.

4 Take your time preparing your meal. Make it special. It doesn't require complex recipes, but it should consist of the very best quality food you can afford, cooked to perfection. As you cook, pour all your hopes and dreams into your chopping and stirring. Believe in the alchemy of culinary magic. You might want to summon a divinity to help you in any desires you may have: Aphrodite for love, Hermes for your career, Athena for wisdom, Zeus for power, and Artemis for travel and freedom.

Take time to list your unique qualities.

Focus on your preparations and imbue them with magic.

5 While your meal is cooking, sit down at your table with a pen and paper. Make a list of all your good qualities – the things you like best about yourself. Then write down all your achievements, however small. Spend a few moments appreciating your very special qualities.

6 Eat your meal with mindfulness and enjoyment. Savor every morsel and take time to relax afterward.

7 Tidy up, taking pleasure in a task well done, then spend the rest of the evening in whatever way you like: perhaps some meditation or yoga, reading a good book, or listening to some favorite music.

You can spend the rest of the evening relaxing in the pleasure of your own company.

FAMILY BONDING: POW-WOW DINNER

VERY FEW FAMILIES FIND THE TIME TO EAT TOGETHER EVERY DAY, YET A SHARED MEAL CAN PROVIDE A STRONG, LOVING FOCUS FOR EVERYONE. THE WHOLE FAMILY SHOULD PULL TOGETHER TO MAKE THE MEAL WORK. CHILDREN MAY GRUMBLE AT FIRST, BUT THEY USUALLY END UP ENJOYING THE SECURITY AND GROUNDING SUCH MEALS GIVE. TRY TO EAT TOGETHER AS A FAMILY AT LEAST ONCE A WEEK, PREFERABLY MORE. THIS RITUAL CAN EASILY BE ADAPTED FOR OCCASIONS WHEN TIME IS SHORT.

YOU WILL NEED

- *Ingredients for a one-pot meal that everyone can help to cook, such as a chili, hotpot, or vegetable stew*
- *A candle for each member of the family — everyone should choose his or her favorite color*
- *Bread*
- *Water and/or wine*
- *A stick or wand*

METHOD

1 Bring everyone together in the kitchen. If you wish, hold hands in a circle and give thanks that you can all be together to eat. Think about families who don't have that luxury, and feel grateful.

2 Share out the work for cooking and preparing. Ideally, let children choose things they enjoy doing. One might decorate the table: encourage the child to be imaginative. Another could gather herbs from the garden. Older children could chop vegetables and herbs. Explain that they are creating "soul food" so they need to imbue their task with loving awareness.

Letting your children help with the preparations will mean that they enjoy the meal more.

3 Everyone can take turns adding herbs or spices to the pot. If they wish, they can say their own magic "spell" as they add the ingredients. This could be something they say out loud or quietly to themselves.

4 Before you serve the food, ask everyone to sit down at the table. Take turns lighting your own candles, making a wish as you do so. This could be something personal, but suggest that it would also be nice to wish for something for the whole family.

5 Place the pot in the center of the table. Think about how all your combined efforts came together to make this one nourishing, delicious pot of food, a caldron of abundance from Mother Earth. Let everyone help themselves to a portion near them.

6 Break bread, pass around the water or wine, and give thanks to the Mother.

7 Eat your meal with mindfulness. Encourage the children to taste and savor their food.

8 After you have finished your meal, sit quietly for a few moments. Place the stick or wand in the center of the table. This is a helpful tool for anyone wanting to get a word in edgeways in large family gatherings! When you have finished sitting quietly, ask everyone to think about anything they may want to say. This is a good time for anyone to bring up matters of concern, any worries and anxieties they may have, or to share good news and happy feelings with the other members of the family.

9 Whoever wishes to speak must hold the "talking stick." While that person speaks, everyone else must listen and not interrupt that person until he or she has put the stick back on the table.

10 When everyone has said what they wanted to say, you should all help to do the dishes.

Each person makes a contribution to the magic of the pot.

Serving each other is a way of showing care and consideration.

CHAPTER FIVE

SPIRITUAL CLEANSING

SPIRITUAL CLEANSING IS AS VITAL AS PHYSICAL WASHING. EACH OF US IS SURROUNDED BY A SPIRITUAL FORCEFIELD CALLED THE "AURA," WHICH SPREADS OUT SEVERAL FEET AROUND US. THE AURA IS AN ELECTROMAGNETIC ENERGY FIELD AND ACTS AS A BUFFER ZONE TO THE OUTSIDE WORLD. IT GIVES US HOARDS OF INFORMATION ABOUT THE WORLD AND OTHER PEOPLE, BUT IT PICKS UP NEGATIVE ENERGY AS WELL AS POSITIVE, SO IT NEEDS CLEANSING TO KEEP IT SHINING BRIGHT.

SENSING YOUR ENERGY FIELD

Try this exercise to feel the magnetic pull of your own energy field.

1 Wash your hands and take off any jewelry, and your watch if you are wearing one. Roll up your sleeves. Sit down with your hands resting on your lap, slightly apart, with your palms facing upward. Gently close your eyes.

2 Relax your hands and, keeping your eyes closed, focus on your palms and fingertips. You may start to feel tiny tingles of electromagnetic energy.

3 Now hold up your hands, palms facing each other, about 12in (30cm) apart. Imagine you are holding a ball. Bounce your palms toward each other, as if you are gently squeezing the ball. You should be able to feel the energy flowing between your hands.

4 Once you can feel the energy, play with it. Take your hands farther apart. How does it feel now? Now bring them closer together. Does the energy feel different in some way?

SEEING YOUR AURA

Most people find that they can see auras to some degree. This technique usually works for people, but it often takes a little practice and patience. If you persevere, you should also be able to distinguish between the colors in your aura.

1 Stand in front of a mirror, at least 18in (45cm) away, and farther if possible. Position yourself in front of the mirror so that you have a white or neutral colored surface behind you, because busy patterns make it difficult to see the aura when you are not used to it. It is also easier if you keep the lighting subdued.

2 Relax, breathe deeply, and look in the mirror. It may help to unfocus your eyes slightly.

3 As you stare past the outline of your head and shoulders, you may start to see a cocoon of light or energy field around your body. If not, try swaying gently from side to side – you should be able to see the energy field moving with you.

4 Can you see any colors in your aura? If not, do you get a feeling about one particular color?

AURA CLEANSING

ONE OF THE BEST THINGS WE CAN DO FOR OURSELVES IS TO KEEP OUR AURAS SHINING CLEAN AND BRIGHT. JUST AS BRUSHING OUR TEETH OR HAVING A BATH IS IMPORTANT FOR OUR PHYSICAL HYGIENE, CLEANSING THE AURA IS ESSENTIAL TO OUR SPIRITUAL WELL-BEING. THERE ARE MANY WAYS TO CLEANSE THE AURA, AND VIRTUALLY EVERY ANCIENT CULTURE HAS ITS OWN TECHNIQUE. THIS VERSION COMBINES ELEMENTS FROM THE NATIVE AMERICAN AND WICCAN TRADITIONS.

YOU WILL NEED

- *Smudge stick, bowl, and a large feather (see page 34), or a light, uplifting incense, or juniper essential oil and oil burner*
- *Matches*
- *Plant mister filled with water, and either a few drops of juniper and lavender essential oils, or a few drops of Bach Rescue Remedy (available from health stores)*
- *Candle*
- *Bowl of sea salt*
- *A blue silk scarf*

METHOD

1 Gather all the ingredients together on a clean table covered with a blue silk scarf.

2 Light the smudge stick, or incense, or oil. Call on the Spirit of Air to cleanse and purify you, and take away negative thoughts.

STEP 2

3 Waft the smoke around your body (if you are using smudge, use the feather to direct the smoke). Pay particular attention to each chakra area (see pages 38–39). Make sure you also cover your back, the bottom of your feet, and the top of your head. You may sense a tingling of energy.

STEP 4

4 Take the mister and spray yourself with a fine spray, calling on the Spirit of Water to take away any negative emotions and feelings. Imagine all the negativity seeping out of your aura and dispersing.

5 Now hold the candle and call on the Spirit of Fire to burn away all the dross and persistent negativity sticking to your aura. Imagine the purifying flames flickering around your body and aura, gently licking them clean.

6 Take a little salt in your hands and touch it, in turn, to each of your chakra centers: the top of your head, your "third eye," your throat, heart, solar plexus, genitals, and base of the spine. Call on the Spirit of Earth to ground you and keep your newly purified aura clean and bright.

7 Stand still, and breathe quietly with your eyes closed. Feel the fresh, clean energy coursing through your body. Thank the elemental spirits for helping you in this cleansing ritual.

8 You may wish to look in the mirror and view your aura – can you detect the difference?

Your aura is an important buffer between you and the outside world.

THE COLORS OF YOUR AURA

Each color has significance in the aura. Here are the main attributes.

PURPLE/VIOLET	Mysticism; deep interest in spirituality.
INDIGO	Inspired thoughts; deep wisdom.
BLUE	Strong mental powers; intelligence; logical thinking.
TURQUOISE	Energy; organization; likes to influence others.
GREEN	Strong sense of balance; deep inner calm; kindness; caring.
DARK GREEN	Deceit or jealousy.
YELLOW	Cheerful personality; joy; freedom; vitality; compassion.
DULL YELLOW	Suspicion; pain; anger.
ORANGE	Vitality; warmth; generosity.
RED	Physical life; vitality; ambition; sexual power.
DARK OR CLOUDY RED	Violent tendencies or hidden anger or rage.
PINK	Love; modesty; gentleness; sometimes shyness.
BROWN	Unsettled; distracted; materialistic; selfish.
GRAY	Depression; low energy; fear.
BLACK	Depression; possibly malice; physical illness or drug abuse.
WHITE	Illness or drug abuse.

SHIELDING THE AURA

OUR AURAS DON'T STAY CLEAN AND BRIGHT FOR LONG. IN THE COURSE OF EVERYDAY LIFE WE MAY MEET UNPLEASANT PEOPLE OR COME ACROSS DIFFICULT SITUATIONS, ALL OF WHICH HAVE A DIRECT UNWELCOME EFFECT ON OUR AURAS. IF OUR AURAS ARE UNPROTECTED, THEY WILL SOON BECOME CLOUDED BY A BUILD-UP OF NEGATIVE ENERGY. LUCKILY THERE ARE SEVERAL SIMPLE TECHNIQUES THAT CAN HELP YOU TO PROTECT YOUR AURA AND STAVE OFF UNWANTED NEGATIVITY.

THE PROTECTIVE BUBBLE

This is a remarkably simple technique, but enormously effective.

1 Relax, and breathe deeply for a few moments.

2 Now imagine a glow of bright, white light deep in your heart chakra.

*Summon up your protective bubble
whenever you are under attack.*

3 As you breathe, the light expands and becomes a shimmering white bubble that grows and grows until it surrounds you entirely. Your body and your aura are now completely cocooned within this glimmering bubble.

4 If you wish, you can change the color of your bubble. Some people like a pure electric blue; others prefer a golden pink. It's up to you.

5 You can also call on any sacred figures to guard your bubble. You may wish to ask the four great archangels to guard each corner (see pages 84–85), or the spirit animals of Native American shamanism (see pages 22–23), or deities from the Egyptian or Hindu pantheon. You could also add meaningful symbols: a cross or a pentagram perhaps?

6 Once you have practiced this technique several times, you will find you can call up your bubble in seconds, whenever you feel the need.

SHIELDING TECHNIQUE

Sometimes we may feel under direct psychic attack. This powerful technique can help.

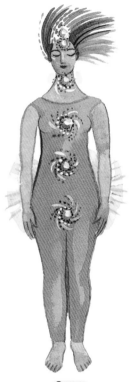

STEP 2

Visualize your chakras spinning with white light.

1   Breathe deeply and turn your attention inward.

2   Visualize all your chakras (see pages 38–39) spinning with white light, like bright shimmering wheels.

3   The wheels spin faster and faster and you may feel a tingle of energy. Then, with a flash, they all join up so that you have a pillar of bright white light within you.

4   Visualize the light flashing out in all directions to fill a rectangular boxlike shape that totally surrounds your body. It is as if you are in a "you-shaped" closet of light.

5   The edges of the light seem to solidify and you know that, on the outside, they have turned into a reflective surface.

6   You are totally safe and comfortable within your box of light, but anyone threatening you will be faced with the dazzling mirrors. Their negativity will simply bounce off the mirrors and be reflected straight back to them.

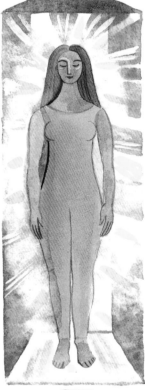

STEP 4

Allow the light to spread out and create a shield around you.

STEP 6

Safe within your shield, all negative forces are repelled from you.

MEDITATION TO CLEANSE THE MIND

OFTEN WE ARE NOT UNDER ATTACK FROM OTHER PEOPLE BUT FROM THE CHAOTIC THOUGHTS OF OUR OWN MINDS. MOST OF US SUFFER FROM "MENTAL POLLUTION," THAT ENDLESS CYCLE OF CONFUSED, WORRIED, HYPERCRITICAL THOUGHTS THAT WE FIND DIFFICULT TO SHUT OFF. MEDITATION IS A SIMPLE WAY OF STARTING TO TAKE CONTROL OVER OUR WAYWARD MINDS SO THAT WE CAN FIND PEACE AND SERENITY IN THE HUBBUB OF EVERYDAY LIFE.

BASIC MEDITATION EXERCISE

KEEP YOUR HEAD, NECK, AND BACK ALIGNED

You will need a firm, supportive chair that is not too high.

1 Sit with an alert and relaxed body posture so that you feel comfortable (either in a straight-backed chair with your feet flat on the floor, or on a thick, firm cushion, three to six inches off the floor).

2 Keep your back straight and aligned with your head and neck, and relax your body.

3 Start to breathe steadily and deeply. Notice your breathing and observe the breath as it flows in and out, feeling your stomach falling and rising. Give it your full attention.

4 If you find your attention starts to wander, simply note the fact and gently bring your thoughts back to your breath, to the rising and falling of your stomach.

5 Try to sit for around 20 minutes at a time. This may take some practice. If you find it difficult at first, just sit for as long as is comfortable, and aim to build up to 20 minutes when you can.

6 Don't jump up immediately afterward. Bring yourself slowly back to normal consciousness. Become aware of the room around you, gently stretch, and "come back" fully before standing up.

OTHER FORMS OF MEDITATION

There are many different ways to meditate. Experiment and see which method works for you.

• Sit in front of a lighted candle. Gently focus your eyes on the candle flame; keep your attention on it. It's okay to blink.

• Slowly count from one to ten in your head, keeping your attention on each number. If you feel your attention wandering, go back and start again. It may help to close your eyes. Don't worry if you can't reach anywhere near ten at first – few people can!

• Choose a mantra – a sacred sound or favorite word or phrase. It might be "Ohm," a vowel sound like "aaaaah," or a phrase like "I am at peace." Choose something meaningful to you. Sit comfortably and repeat your chosen phrase for as long as you can: 20 minutes is ideal, but even 5 minutes will suffice.

• Use the sound meditation given on pages 38–39.

• If you find the idea of meditation uncomfortable, try Autogenic Training instead, a Westernized form of meditation that trains you to relax the muscles and organs of your body. Your local natural health center should be able to help.

• Remember that mindfulness is a form of meditation too. Recap by reading pages 12–13.

Twenty minutes is long enough for you to cleanse your mind.

Give your attention to a candle flame to break the cycle of confused thoughts.

Ohm

I am at peace

Repeating a soothing sound will help to empty your mind.

Use an affirmation to focus your mind and body.

AFTER AN
ARGUMENT CLEANSING

ARGUMENTS AND DISAGREEMENTS HAPPEN TO US ALL. WHETHER IT IS A FULL-SCALE ROW OR AN UNPLEASANT SPAT, ARGUMENTS INEVITABLY LEAVE US FEELING LOW OR UNEASY. IT'S NOT SURPRISING: WHEN WE BECOME ANGRY WITH SOMEONE, OUR AURA IS DISTURBED AND NEGATIVITY SEEPS THROUGH INTO EVERY CELL OF OUR BODIES. SO AFTER AN ARGUMENT IT IS ESSENTIAL THAT WE SPEND SOME TIME "CLEARING THE AIR" AND REPAIRING THE PSYCHIC DAMAGE.

YOU WILL NEED

- *Pine essential oil, oil burner, and matches*
- *White candle*
- *Beech flower remedy (available from health stores)*
- *Paper and pen*
- *Squeaky toy or party squeaker*

METHOD

1 Light the oil burner and add two drops of pine essential oil to the water reservoir. Pine fosters forgiveness and fair-mindedness. The two drops represent the two of you involved in the argument. If there are more of you, add more drops accordingly. Also light the candle.

STEP 1

2 Sit or lie down, and breathe calmly and deeply for a few minutes. Feel the clean scent of pine start to make the reasons for the conflict clearer.

STEP 2

Find a calm space in which to review your feelings.

3 Put two drops of Beech flower remedy under your tongue. Beech helps to resolve bitterness and anger, and it stops you from being overcritical.

STEP 4

4 Write down the reasons for your argument. You can pour out all your resentment and any lingering feelings of anger.

Use the blank page as a target for your resentment.

You didn't bother to ask m how I felt about it: yo just presumed I didn't mind. You were too wrapped up in your ow concerns to notice what was going on. And when I tried talk to you abou you didn't hav time to listen

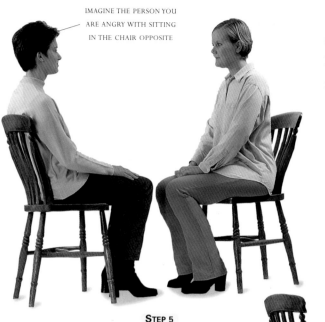

IMAGINE THE PERSON YOU
ARE ANGRY WITH SITTING
IN THE CHAIR OPPOSITE

STEP 5

9 Finally, take the toy or party squeaker and squeak it all around your aura. The happy, silly sound will shake away any remaining vestiges of negativity.

NOW SWAP CHAIRS AND TRY TO
IMAGINE HOW THE OTHER PERSON
IS FEELING

STEP 6

5 Can you see the other person's point of view? If you still find this impossible, take two chairs. Sit on one chair and imagine the other person is sitting on the other chair. Explain exactly why you were feeling so angry.

6 Now swap chairs and imagine you are the other person. What made him or her angry? Allow yourself to slip into that person's shoes and express his or her grievances. If necessary, you can keep swapping chairs until you can clearly see and understand both sides of the situation.

7 Try to accept that there are two sides to every argument. Even if you still disagree with the other person, decide that you will be forgiving. Burn the piece of paper containing your grievances.

8 Visualize love and forgiveness shooting out from your heart chakra to that of the other person. Imagine it as a beautiful pink-gold color.

8 Add two more drops of pine oil to the oil burner (or more if there are more people involved), and imagine the drops of oil joining peacefully as one.

STEP 9

BLOW THE SQUEAKER
TO GET RID OF ALL
THE NEGATIVE ENERGY

DEEP CLEANSING BATH AND PURIFYING SHOWER

WATER IS DEEPLY CLEANSING AND PURIFYING, SO IT MAKES SENSE TO USE YOUR REGULAR BATH OR SHOWER AS A TOOL FOR SOME POWERFUL SPIRITUAL CLEANSING. THE PURIFYING SHOWER SHOWN HERE IS THE PERFECT WAY TO START YOUR DAY, AND WILL MAKE YOU FEEL INVIGORATED, POSITIVE, AND UPBEAT. THE DEEP CLEANSING BATH IS SOOTHING, AND IDEAL FOR SHEDDING THE TRIALS AND TRIBULATIONS OF A STRESSFUL DAY.

PURIFYING SHOWER

YOU WILL NEED

♦ *Pine and juniper essential oils*

Fresh running water is the most natural cleanser there is.

METHOD

1 Spend a few moments focusing on your breathing. Stretch upward as far as you can, as if you were trying to touch the sky. Feel yourself become taller and looser.

2 Adjust the water in your shower to a cool temperature. Make it as cool as is comfortable. Put two drops each of the pine and juniper oils on your sponge or facecloth.

3 Step into the shower. Imagine you are stepping under the clean, pure waters of a beautiful waterfall somewhere in the wilderness. As you stand under the waters, tell yourself that the magical water is washing away any negativity.

4 Wash yourself with the sponge and smell the fresh, uplifting scent of the essential oils. They bring to mind the tall guardian trees of the woodland that could surround your magical waterfall.

5 Let go of any worries. Affirm that the day ahead will be positive and full of joy. Any problems will be challenges that you will overcome with ease.

6 Step out of the shower, return to normal consciousness, and enjoy your day.

DEEP CLEANSING BATH

YOU WILL NEED

- Candles or night lights
- Oil burner (optional)
- Sandalwood and geranium essential oils
- Bundle of herbs (rosemary, sage, basil, lavender)
- Sea salt
- Rose petals (optional)

Bring the stress and negativity of the day to your bathing space and allow it to fall away.

CAUTION

Consult a qualified aromatherapist before using essential oils for children or pregnant women, or those with a serious medical condition.

METHOD

1 Light candles all around your bathtub. If you wish, you can also light an oil burner and put three drops each of the sandalwood and geranium oils into the water reservoir.

2 Run your bath to the correct temperature. It should be pleasantly warm but not too hot. While the water is running, tie the bundle of herbs so that the water runs through it. Add three drops each of sandalwood and geranium oils to the water and disperse them. Add the rose petals, if using.

3 As you take off your clothes, imagine that you are dropping your everyday persona and that you are starting to let go of the stress, strain, and negativity of the day.

CAUTION

Before doing steps 4 and 5, consult your physician if you have high blood pressure or heart disease.

4 Sprinkle some sea salt onto a damp facecloth. Gently scrub your body with small circular movements. Start at your heart and work outward.

5 Spend a few moments imagining the purifying power of the sea salt loosening all the psychic grime of the day.

6 Lie in the bath and visualize the healing water gently drawing out all the negativity and unpleasantness of the day. You should soak for at least twenty minutes.

7 Take the herb bundle and gently scrub your body with it to get rid of any remaining dross. Imagine the herbs scrubbing away any impurities.

8 As you step out of the bath, look back and envisage the water carrying away all the stress and tension of the day.

9 Say a word of thanks to the water and herbs. Now you should find that you sleep well and awake rested and refreshed.

CHAPTER SIX

RELEASING NEGATIVE ENERGY

SOME PEOPLE AND PLACES SEEM TO DRAG US DOWN, AS IF THEY EXUDE A NEGATIVE CHARGE OF ENERGY. IN FACT THEY DO JUST THAT. CERTAIN PEOPLE CAN BE PSYCHIC "VAMPIRES," SUCKING OUT ALL OUR ENERGY AND JOIE DE VIVRE. PLACES CAN HAVE THE SAME EFFECT. OUR OWN NEGATIVE THOUGHTS CAN ALSO SAP OUR ENERGY. HOWEVER, THERE ARE TECHNIQUES FOR SHIELDING OURSELVES FROM THESE ENERGY DRAINS SO THAT WE CAN RELEASE NEGATIVE ENERGY SWIFTLY AND SAFELY.

PSYCHIC VAMPIRES

We've all met people who leave us drained. We walk away from the encounter feeling depressed or sad for no apparent reason. These "psychic vampires" don't generally mean to pull you down, they just happen to be the kind of people who have the capacity to pull energy from you. Often they carry around a deep level of negativity: they tend to cast themselves in the role of victim and may bombard you with stories of the ills the world pours upon them. They do not take responsibility for their own lives or their own energy. There is little you can do to change such people – they have to make that decision for themselves. But you need to protect yourself so that you do not take on their woes.

ENERGY DRAINS

Has a place ever made you feel uncomfortable or uneasy? Some buildings and rooms, for instance, can soak up the feelings and moods of the people who inhabit them. If a place has seen constant arguing, violence, or unhappiness, those negative emotions will remain buried in the walls, in the very energetic structure of the place, and can build up over the years. Our auras pick up the uncomfortable energy patterns and we, in turn, feel uneasy. While you may not be able to do a full space cleansing in every building you occupy, there are ways to create a safe space for the duration of your visit.

OUR OWN NEGATIVITY

We can't always blame other people and places for our feelings of negativity. Often we need to release ourselves from our own destructive patterns of behavior or obsessive, negative thoughts. If we let our guard down, we can find that simple everyday problems can turn into monsters and destroy our self-esteem and equilibrium. The techniques that follow will help to deal with such thoughts and emotions before they spiral out of control.

CREATING SAFE SPACE

IMAGINE YOU ARE STAYING IN A HOTEL, OR SPENDING THE NIGHT AT A FRIEND'S HOME, AND SOMETHING FEELS WRONG WITH YOUR ROOM. SOME PLACES ARE SIMPLY NOT CONDUCIVE TO RESTFUL SLEEP AND RELAXATION. WHILE IT MAY BE IMPRACTICAL — OR IMPOLITE — TO CARRY OUT A FULL SPACE CLEANSING, THIS POWERFUL RITUAL WILL CREATE A SAFE SPACE FOR YOU FOR THE DURATION OF YOUR STAY. IT IS BASED ON A CABALISTIC PROTECTION CEREMONY.

YOU WILL NEED

◆ *Just yourself*

METHOD

1 Stand in the center of the room. Spend a few moments becoming aware of your breathing, then ground and center yourself (see page 31).

2 Build up a bubble of protection (see page 74). Send the bubble out farther to encompass the entire room. Imagine the pure white light searching out every shadow and every scrap of negative energy, sending them scurrying away from the force of the light.

3 Now call on the four great archangels, powerful forces who can protect you and keep you safe whenever you feel uneasy.

4 First summon Raphael, the archangel of the East, who will stand in front of you. Intone his name aloud or silently, breaking it into syllables

Raphael's face blazes like the morning sun.

Creating a bubble of protection gives you a secure and powerful center.

– *Ra-fay-ell* – over and over. Imagine this great healer clothed in robes of amber and gold. His face shines brightly like the sun, and you know he will allow nothing to approach you from the East.

5 Now summon Gabriel, archangel of the West, who will stand behind you and guard your back. Intone his name – *Ga-bree-ell* – over and over, until you feel his presence. Gabriel is the great messenger, clad in robes of violet and silver. He shines like the moon. You are safe with Gabriel behind you.

Summon Gabriel to stand behind you.

The stern and beautiful Uriel is a strong protector.

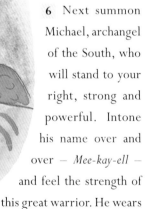

Michael is the great and powerful warrior of heaven.

6 Next summon Michael, archangel of the South, who will stand to your right, strong and powerful. Intone his name over and over – *Mee-kay-ell* – and feel the strength of this great warrior. He wears a beautiful glowing orange cloak over his golden armor, which shimmers and glows with power.

7 Finally, summon Uriel, archangel of the North, who will stand to your left, wise and protecting. Intone his name – *Ur-ee-ell* – over and over. Uriel is incredibly tall and wears flowing robes of black and yellow. His face is stern but beautiful. You will feel secure with him beside you.

8 Once you have greeted the four great archangels, they will turn away from you to set up their guard. Now you can relax, knowing you are safe. However, if at any point you feel uneasy, simply repeat their names in sequence, until you feel comfortable.

CUTTING TIES

WHILE IT IS GOOD AND NECESSARY TO HAVE LOVING LINKS WITH PEOPLE, ALL TOO OFTEN WE ARE BOUND TO OTHERS BY LESS HEALTHY EMOTIONS. MANY OF US ARE TIED BY GUILT, DUTY, LUST, OR HABIT. OTHERS ARE TIED TO MORE DESTRUCTIVE RELATIONSHIPS BASED ON FEAR, POWER, OR ANGER. THIS RITUAL CAN HELP YOU TO RELEASE YOURSELF FROM A DEPENDENT OR DESTRUCTIVE RELATIONSHIP. IT NEED NOT END YOUR RELATIONSHIP, BUT MAY WELL TRANSFORM IT.

YOU WILL NEED

◆ *Just yourself*

METHOD

1 Sit or stand quietly and become aware of your breathing. Ground and center yourself (see page 31).

2 Now imagine yourself in a bubble of pure white light (see page 74). Let it extend to about 6ft (1.8m) around you. Be aware that, while you are inside this protective bubble, nothing and no one can hurt or harm you.

3 Now think about the person to whom you feel tied. You may feel uncomfortable or uneasy but just stay with that feeling, knowing you are safe.

4 Visualize a second bubble of light a short distance from yours. The other person is inside, kept firmly in place by the bubble.

5 Observe the person – what is he or she doing? Trying to talk to you perhaps? What is being said?

6 Remember that you are in control. If you want to talk to this person, to understand your relationship better, or to state your case, take turns speaking. However unreasonable the person may be in normal life, in this situation he or she will listen to you. Say what you feel, what you have always wanted to say.

A THIN SILVER CORD STRETCHES BETWEEN YOU

STEP 4

Examine your destructive relationship from the security of your protective bubble.

7 When you have finished speaking or observing, notice that you have a thin, silver cord that stretches from your solar plexus to the other person's solar plexus. Give it a small tug and notice the other person lurch toward you slightly. This is the source of your attachment.

8 The time has come to cut this attachment, to release both of you from this form of relationship. Remember that it does not mean that you cannot continue to have a relationship: it will just be different, and more as you wish it to be. If you wish, you can build a new relationship based on equality, mutual respect, and fairness.

9 Visualize yourself picking up a pair of silver scissors. Before you sever your current relationship, send love, forgiveness, and understanding – as far as you are able – to the other person. Then cut the cord, saying: "I release us from this negative pattern of relationship. Now we are safe."

10 Notice that the cord shimmers and is then absorbed back into your solar plexus. Now you both stand free in your bubbles.

11 Does the situation feel any different? What do you notice about the person now? How does your solar plexus feel? Take a few moments to consider your feelings about what has just happened.

12 Come back to full waking awareness. To refresh yourself, stamp your feet, have a hot drink, and perhaps eat a cookie.

STEP 9

After you have explored your feelings about the relationship, you will be empowered to cut the cord that holds you in subjection.

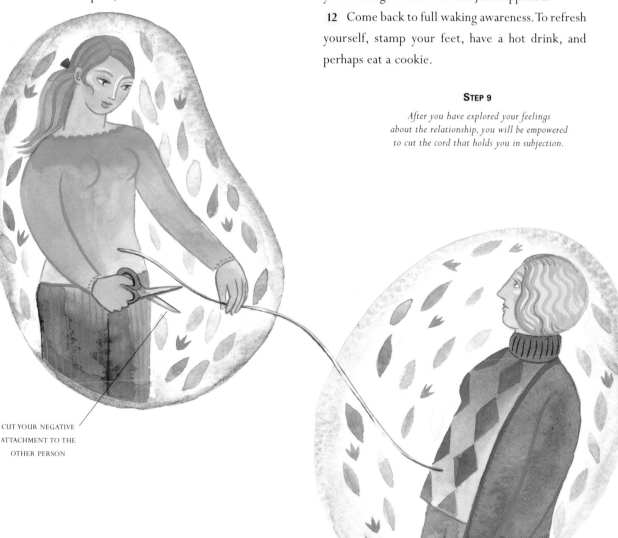

CUT YOUR NEGATIVE
ATTACHMENT TO THE
OTHER PERSON

RELEASING YOURSELF
FROM PROBLEMS

PROBLEMS, WHETHER LARGE OR SMALL, CAN GROW OUT OF CONTROL. BEFORE
WE KNOW WHERE WE ARE, THEY HAVE EXPANDED TO THE POINT WHERE THEY
DOMINATE OUR LIVES, MAKING US ANXIOUS AND WORRIED WHILE WE ARE AWAKE,
AND TURNING OUR DREAMS INTO NIGHTMARES WHILE WE SLEEP. THIS RITUAL CAN
HELP YOU TO PUT YOUR PROBLEMS INTO PERSPECTIVE AND ALLOW YOU TO RELEASE
THE ENERGY THAT GIVES THEM CONTROL OVER YOU.

YOU WILL NEED

- *2 sheets of paper
  and a pen*
- *Freezerproof bowl
  or container*
- *Lavender essential oil*

METHOD

1 Sit down quietly and spend a few moments,
as always, focusing on your breathing. Ground and
center yourself (see page 31).

2 Think about your problem, then write it at the
top of a sheet of paper. Underneath put down all
the elements of the problem. What are your major
concerns? What is the worst thing that could

happen as a result of this problem? What is your
greatest fear? Write down every negative thought
and feeling you have – the more the better.

3 Now you are going to put your problem on ice
– literally. This will leave your mind free to come
up with some more positive approaches to the
problem. Put the piece of paper in a freezerproof
container and fill it with water. Add three drops of
lavender essential oil – lavender helps you to release
and let go of any worries.

*Get ready to put the problem
to one side for a time.*

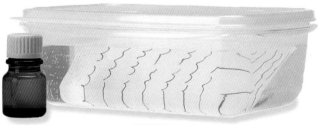

STEP 3

4 Now put the container in the freezer and leave
it until the water is completely solid.

5 When the water is frozen, take the container
out of the freezer. Remove the ice that contains the
paper (you may need to use a little warm water).

STEP 2

*Write down all the different
aspects of your problem.*

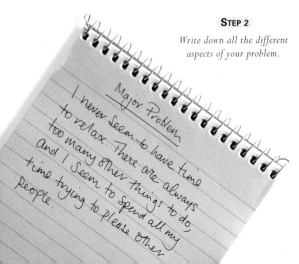

Major Problem

I never seem to have time
to relax. There are always
too many other things to do,
and I seem to spend all my
time trying to please other
people.

6 Set the ice on a large plate or dish, then bring it into a warm room. Place it in front of you on a table, then sit down and watch it melt. As it melts, visualize all the difficulties and anxiety melting away. This problem has no power over you anymore. You may well find, as you watch the ice melting, that you start to have more constructive thoughts and ideas about the problem. Take a fresh sheet of paper and write them down. The piece of paper that contains the old problem can now be thrown away.

STEP 4

Visualize your difficulties being held within the ice in the container.

STEP 6

As the power of your anxieties melts with the ice, write down the positive solutions that come to you.

Constructive thoughts
I need to sit down and make a list of tasks, and cross off any that I don't really want to do, or that have outlived their usefulness. Perhaps I can get people to help? Then I'll prioritize the rest and deal with them in order.

RELEASING NEGATIVE THOUGHTS

ARE YOU OBSESSED WITH NEGATIVE THOUGHTS ABOUT YOURSELF: YOUR BODY, YOUR ABILITIES, YOUR SELF-WORTH? IT IS EASY TO FALL INTO THE TRAP OF LISTENING TO THE "INNER CRITIC," THE CARPING, CRITICAL VOICE THAT SOMETIMES SEEMS TO TAKE OVER YOUR MIND. SUCH NEGATIVITY NEEDS TO BE WEEDED OUT, FIRMLY AND DECISIVELY. USE THIS RITUAL TO HELP BREAK THE CYCLE OF NEGATIVE SELF-CRITICISM.

YOU WILL NEED

- *Mandarin essential oil, and oil burner*
- *Matches*
- *Several sheets of paper and a pen*
- *Two small mirrors of similar size and shape*
- *Green ribbon*

I'm not good enough

I feel guilty

A negative self-image can blight and poison our daily lives.

METHOD

1 Light the oil burner and put four drops of mandarin essential oil in the water reservoir. Mandarin helps to foster self-esteem and positive thoughts.

2 Think about your most negative thought. What is it? Common ones are "I'm fat and ugly"; "I'm not good enough"; "I feel guilty"; "I hate myself"; "I'm a lousy mother/friend/son." Pick the one that really strikes a chord with you. Write it on a piece of paper,

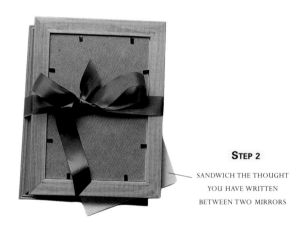

STEP 2

SANDWICH THE THOUGHT
YOU HAVE WRITTEN
BETWEEN TWO MIRRORS

then put it between mirrors of similar size with their reflective surfaces facing inward. Tie a piece of green ribbon around the mirrors and put them in a safe place.

3 Now think of a statement that is exactly the opposite of your negative thought. It could be something like "My body is ideal for me"; "I am just fine in everything I do"; "I forgive myself completely"; "I am a wonderful mother/friend/son." If you recoil from this new thought then congratulate yourself – you've hit on the perfect statement.

4 Write down your new positive statement on a sheet of paper. Next to it write down your immediate reaction, which may be something like "what a load of rubbish." Continue writing your positive statement twenty times, each time noting your responses. You may write a line or several pages – let your mind free-associate and you could be surprised at what emerges.

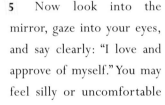

STEP 4

Record your responses to a positive statement about yourself.

5 Now look into the mirror, gaze into your eyes, and say clearly: "I love and approve of myself." You may feel silly or uncomfortable saying this at first, but persevere. Repeat it out loud to yourself at least ten times.

6 For the very best results, you should repeat this ritual every day for 21 days. During this time you will probably find that your relationship with yourself and your thoughts starts to change. You may also discover some interesting and perhaps even unknown factors relating to your negativity about yourself. At the end of the 21 days you can untie the mirrors and burn the old negative thought – you don't need it anymore.

Look into the mirror with a positive view of yourself.

BANISHING OBSESSIVE THOUGHTS

If you suffer from repetitive thoughts or worries that swirl around your head and prevent you from resting or sleeping, try putting three drops of White Chestnut Bach flower remedy (available from health stores) under your tongue. Then, every time the thought surfaces, imagine a large red STOP sign in your head that drives the negative thought away. You can also firmly say "Stop!" or "Go away!" either out loud or silently.

VISUALIZE THE NEGATIVE
CYCLE CEASING

CHAPTER SEVEN

SACRED SEXUALITY

OUR SEXUALITY IS A SACRED GIFT. WHEN WE MAKE LOVE WITH CONSCIOUS AWARENESS, WE CAN TRANSFORM OUR BODIES INTO TEMPLES OF THE SPIRIT. OVER THE CENTURIES ANCIENT CULTURES HAVE TAUGHT THAT SEXUALITY AND SENSUALITY ARE GIFTS OF GOD AND CAN TAKE US AS CLOSE TO THE DIVINE AS ANY FORM OF PRAYER OR MEDITATION. THERE ARE MANY THINGS WE CAN DO TO BRING A SENSE OF THE SACRED INTO OUR SEX LIVES.

The idea of sacred sexuality is nothing new. For thousands of years sexuality has been venerated as a gift from God and a way of coming closer to the divine. Most ancient cultures considered lovemaking an art to be cultivated and it was taken extremely seriously.

It has only been in the last few hundred years that we have seen sex as something almost diametrically opposed to the divine. The Western Christian Church tried hard to suppress the joy of sex, claiming that intercourse was only intended for procreation and that any enjoyment of sex was lustful and the work of the devil. This reached a head in the nineteenth century when prudery became so intense that even the legs of chairs were covered so that their "bare limbs" would not provoke lust.

In the 1960s a backlash occurred with books and magazines reasserting the joy of sensual experience. However, in the last thirty years we have witnessed sex becoming almost a commodity, a skill to be learned, and prowess to be boasted about. We have been encouraged to have bigger, better orgasms; to

try more bizarre positions; to experiment with "wonder" sex pills. Nowadays sex is increasingly being seen as the pursuit of pleasure and rarely as a path to the sacred.

REDISCOVERING THE JOY OF SEX

Reclaiming sexuality as a link with the sacred can take a large leap of the imagination and a complete readjustment of our habits. First of all we have to accept that our bodies are beautiful, whatever perceptions society has foisted on us, and that they can be gateways to exquisite pleasure and the joy of both physical and mystical union. We must accept that sex is a precious gift: when we join with another person in conscious, sacred, sexual union, we replay the divine alchemy of creation. By learning to be aware of our sensuality and gaining control of our physical responses, we can turn lovemaking into something approaching divine ecstasy – union with God. This is the aim of all the great ancient traditions of sexuality, from Tantra to the Tao.

THE GREAT MYSTICAL TRADITIONS OF SACRED SEX

FROM TANTRA TO THE TAO, FROM THE CABALA TO THE KAMA SUTRA, THE GREAT ANCIENT CULTURES OF THE WORLD HAVE ALWAYS INCORPORATED SEXUAL TEACHINGS AND TECHNIQUES INTO THEIR CREEDS. SEXUALITY WAS NEVER DISMISSED AS MERE FUN OR FROLIC: IT WAS CONSIDERED TO BE AN ART. STUDENTS OF SACRED SEX WOULD SPEND YEARS LEARNING HOW TO CONTROL THEIR BODIES, THOUGHTS, AND FEELINGS IN ORDER TO ATTAIN THEIR GOAL — UNION WITH GOD.

TANTRA – THE RELIGION OF SEX

Throughout its 6,000 year history, Tantra has remained for the most part a hidden path, taught by gurus to carefully selected disciples. It has been much misunderstood, even in its native India, where traditional Hindus frowned upon many of its seemingly bizarre practices.

Traditionally, Tantric belief claims that the raw power of the sexual urge can be transformed into the spiritual energy necessary to reach *Nirvana*, or union with God. The follower of Tantra believes that the universe comprises pairs of polar opposites and it is this duality that causes all sorrow and suffering. The original state of the universe was one of joyous unity, symbolized by the endless intercourse of the female and male deities (Shakti and Shiva), so the ultimate

The god Shiva with the Wives of Sages in an eighteenth-century painting. The Tantric tradition of India views human sexuality as a sacred enactment of the divine unity of the universe.

aim of the Tantric couple is to reproduce that divine union on a human scale. Therefore, true Tantric sex becomes both a meditation and a sacrament.

THE KAMA SUTRA – CELEBRATING SENSUALITY

The Kama Sutra also has its origins in India, but it was far more generally accepted. The original text was produced between 100CE and 400CE and aimed to teach the union of body, mind, and spirit through the joy of sex. It stressed the importance of cultivating all five senses. Making love was considered an art form of the highest degree, as refined as good art, fine music, or *haute cuisine*.

Nowadays, we tend to consider the Kama Sutra as a book of bizarre and limb-contorting sexual postures – a bit of a joke perhaps. But many of the positions are actually based on yoga postures, with the aim of aligning mind and body, bringing the soul into balance. It's therefore well worth studying the Kama Sutra with a fresh eye.

Taoist teachings emphasize the importance of sex to overall well-being.

This sculpture on the facade of a Hindu temple in Madhya Pradesh showing Vishnu and Lakshmi embracing suggests the importance of sex in Indian religious traditions.

THE TAO – THE CHINESE PATH TO SEXUAL WISDOM

No one can tell precisely when the Tao of Sex came into being. Like much of Chinese culture, its origins are shrouded in the mists of antiquity, and it stretches back many thousands of years. Taoists believe that sex is a vital part of good health. Using sexual energy in specific ways can improve your health, strengthen your relationships, and bring you closer to the sacred. Taoist lovemaking is a highly refined art form.

DEDICATING YOUR BEDROOM

YOUR BEDROOM SHOULD BE A PLACE OF SENSUAL DELIGHT, A REFUGE FROM THE
OUTSIDE WORLD. IT SHOULD MAKE YOU RELAX AND FEEL GOOD THE MOMENT YOU
WALK THROUGH THE DOOR, YET MANY OF US PAY LITTLE ATTENTION TO THE ROOM
WE USE FOR SLEEPING, DREAMING, AND MAKING LOVE. OFTEN BEDROOMS ARE
CLUTTERED AND MESSY, WITH LITTLE THOUGHT GIVEN TO THEIR DESIGN, BUT A
FEW SIMPLE STEPS CAN TRANSFORM THEM INTO PLACES OF SENSUAL DELIGHT.

PRACTICAL STEPS

1 First clear out all the clutter. Make sure there is nothing in your bedroom that does not relate to sleep, sex, or relaxation, so banish televisions, computers, and work-related mess.

2 Introduce rich, luxurious coverings, cushions, and pillows in pinks and reds. Velvet, satin, and silk are exotic fabrics. Fake fur can be very sensual – how about a huge fake fur for your bed?

3 Lighting should be soft and sensual. Stock up on plenty of pink and red candles.

4 Scent your room with exotic, sensual fragrances. Try sandalwood, neroli, ylang ylang, patchouli, lavender, and jasmine.

5 Have massage oils ready-mixed by the bed so they are at hand when you need them. Once you have prepared your room, you are ready to perform this simple dedication ritual.

Gather the accessories you will need to transform your sleeping space.

LUXURIOUS CUSHIONS AND COVERINGS IN PINK SILKS

MAKE SURE YOU HAVE PLENTY OF PINK AND RED CANDLES

MASSAGE OILS

YOU WILL NEED

◆ *Incense, or a smudge stick with a bowl and a large feather (see page 34)*

◆ *Matches*

◆ *A red candle*

METHOD

1 Light the incense or smudge stick, then waft the smoke to cleanse spiritually every part of the room (see page 34).

2 Stand in the middle of the room and breathe. Become aware of your chakras, the spinning wheels of energy in your body (see pages 38–39).

3 Focus on the genital chakra and see it glowing a deep orange-red. Feel it pulsing with the rhythm of life and the earth.

4 Now bring your awareness to your heart chakra, pulsing with the pure green vigor of life. Feel the love you possess within you and avow your intent to use that love wisely and carefully.

5 Next bring your awareness up into the crown of your head where energy swirls in beautiful waves of violet and pure white. Recognize the pure spirituality of this chakra, its closeness to the sacred and to God.

6 Now imagine all three chakras linked to each other. Recognize that spirituality, emotional love, and physical sensuality are all manifestations of the sacred, all part of the whole.

7 Visualize the three energies joining together in a ball of beautiful, vibrant, loving energy. Throw this ball out to spread through your room, sending with it a prayer that in this room you will dedicate yourself to exploring the sacredness of love and sex.

8 When you have finished, stamp your feet to refresh yourself and then bring yourself back to normal waking awareness.

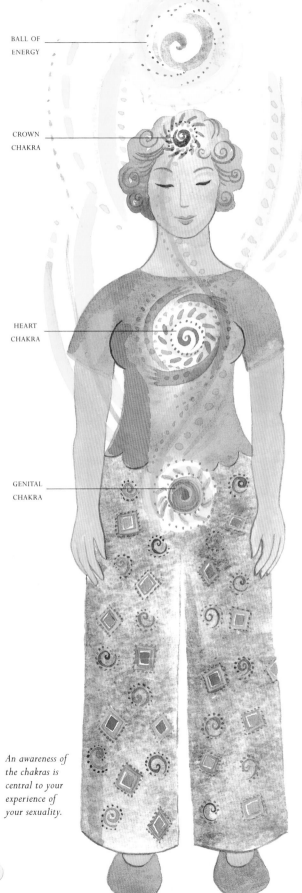

BALL OF ENERGY

CROWN CHAKRA

HEART CHAKRA

GENITAL CHAKRA

An awareness of the chakras is central to your experience of your sexuality.

CULTIVATING SENSUALITY

BEFORE YOU CAN TRULY TURN SEX INTO A SACRED ACT, YOU NEED TO BECOME FULLY AWAKE TO YOUR OWN WONDROUS SENSUALITY. FEW OF US TAKE THE TIME AND EFFORT TO EXPLORE OUR OWN BODIES — AND THOSE OF OUR PARTNERS — WITH ANYWHERE NEAR THE LOVE AND AWE THEY DESERVE. THESE EXERCISES WILL HELP TO PUT YOU BACK IN TOUCH WITH YOUR BODY, SO THAT YOU CAN BRING SACREDNESS BACK INTO YOUR LOVEMAKING.

BECOMING AWARE OF YOUR OWN BODY

This exercise makes you aware of every part of your body. If you feel out of touch with your body or, like most of us, could do with improving your relationship with your body, then this technique should work wonders.

YOU WILL NEED

◆ *Loose clothing*

METHOD

1 Lie on the floor on your back. Become aware of your body lying on the floor: feel the floor under you and where it supports your body.

2 Now put your attention into your feet: imagine the bones of your feet, the muscles, the tendons, the skin. Are they hot or cold? Do you feel any difference between your two feet? Are they light or heavy?

3 Now gradually work up your body, repeating the questions, becoming aware of how different parts of your body feel. Move up your legs into your hips, up your torso, and down your arms. End with your head and face.

4 Now, using either your fingers or lightly clenched fists, swiftly tap over your hip bones and pelvis. Listen to the sounds they make and feel the vibrations in your body.

5 Move down your legs, and listen and feel for changes in sound and feeling. Try the soles of your feet. Work over all the bones in your body, noting differences.

Sexual fulfillment begins with an awareness of our own bodies.

START WITH YOUR FEET — ARE THEY HOT OR COLD?

MOVE UP YOUR BODY — LEGS, HIPS, TORSO, THEN DOWN YOUR ARMS

END WITH YOUR HEAD AND FACE

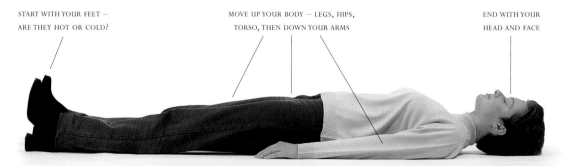

DISCOVERING
YOUR PARTNER'S BODY

You should practice this exercise with your partner. It will teach you both how to increase the sensuality in your life. When we have sex, we often tend to think of touching just the prime erogenous zones: this exercise reminds us that other parts of our bodies can also be very receptive.

1 Make sure you will not be disturbed, and then take off your clothes, soften the lights, and play soothing music.

2 Sit down facing each other, then start to explore your partner's face with your fingertips and lips. You should spend about five minutes doing this.

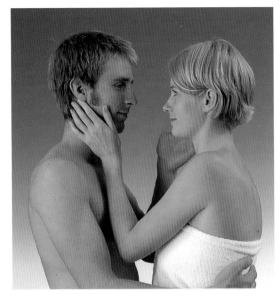

STEP 3

Make eye contact with your partner as you touch each other.

STEP 4

Try to discover where your partner's body is most sensitive.

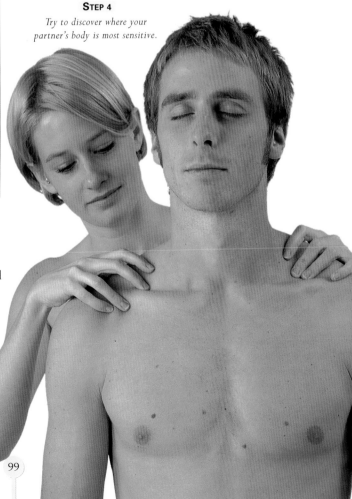

STEP 2

The face is full of sensitive nerve endings that respond to touch.

3 Swap over and enjoy being on the receiving end of your partner's exploration.

4 Next move on to the whole body, exploring everywhere except breasts and genitals. Ask your partner for feedback: stroke, massage, caress, and kiss the areas your partner tells you have the most sensation.

SENSUAL MASSAGE FOR LOVERS

MASSAGE IS ONE OF THE BEST WAYS TO RELAX, TO LET GO OF THE DAY, AND FORM A DEEP EMOTIONAL BOND WITH YOUR PARTNER. IT ALSO GIVES YOU THE CHANCE TO FOCUS YOUR SENSES AND TO BECOME DEEPLY AWARE OF YOUR PARTNER'S BODY. THIS SIMPLE MASSAGE DOESN'T NEED TO BE PERFECT OR PROFESSIONAL: GO BY YOUR INSTINCTS AND KEEP CHECKING FOR RESPONSES SO THAT YOU CAN GIVE YOUR PARTNER A MASSAGE THAT HE OR SHE WILL REALLY ENJOY.

YOU WILL NEED

- *3 candles (perhaps pink for romance, orange for friendship, and red for passion, or choose colors to suit your own taste)*
- *Relaxing music*
- *6 drops sandlewood or ylang ylang essential oil, plus extra for oil burner, if using*
- *Oil burner (optional)*
- *4 tsp (20ml) base oil, such as sweet almond*

METHOD

1 Light the candles and put on some background music to help you relax. You may also like to light an oil burner and add some sensual oil, such as sandalwood or ylang ylang, to the water reservoir.

STEP 3

Start the massage near the base of the spine, then work up to the shoulders.

2 Make up your massage oil by mixing 6 drops of essential oil with the base oil.

3 Start massaging your partner's back with your thumbs on either side of the spine; your fingers should be pointing toward the neck. Allow your hands to glide slowly up the body and around the shoulders. Draw your hands lightly down the sides and then return to your starting position. You don't have to be an expert in massage. Just remember to keep a slow, steady rhythm with the right amount of pressure for your partner.

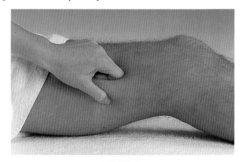

STEP 4

Using your fingers and thumb, knead fleshy areas such as hips and thighs.

4 Gently knead fleshy areas, such as hips and thighs. Lift, squeeze, and roll the skin between the thumb and fingers of one hand and glide it toward the other hand.

5 Curl your fingers into loose fists, keeping the fingers, not the knuckles, against the skin. Work your fists all over your partner's body.

STEP 5
Keep your fists against your partner's skin as you work around the body.

6 Using your fingertips, make small circling movements on the shoulders, palms of the hands, soles of the feet, and the chest.

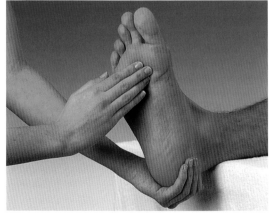

STEP 6
Use your fingertips to give a gentle massage to sensitive areas of the body.

7 Form your hands into cup shapes. Using quick, light movements, move over the skin as if you are beating a drum.

STEP 7
Light, beating movements are invigorating and refreshing.

8 Be inventive, and let your partner's responses guide you. You could use your whole body to massage your partner, or trail your hair over your partner's body. Try scratching your partner lightly.

9 As you reach the end of your sensual massage, revive your partner with some light pummeling: make your hands into loose fists and lightly bounce the sides of your hands alternately against the skin.

STEP 8
Use your instincts, and let your partner's reactions be your guide.

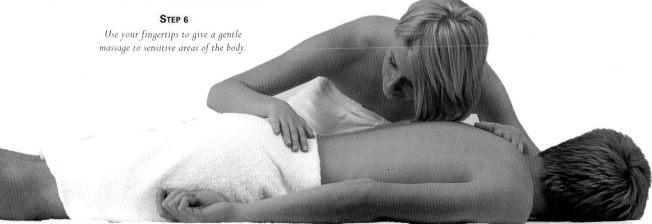

TANTRIC MAITHUNA

THE TANTRIC ART OF LOVEMAKING HAS MANY RITUALS. ADEPTS CAN SPEND YEARS AND YEARS PRACTICING VISUALIZATION, BREATHING, MEDITATION, AND PRACTICAL LOVEMAKING, SO YOU CAN'T EXPECT TO BECOME A TANTRIC ADEPT OVERNIGHT. HOWEVER, THIS RITUAL CAN INTRODUCE YOU TO SOME OF THE CONCEPTS AND TECHNIQUES OF THE SACRED ART OF SEXUALITY. IT IS BASED ON THE TANTRIC CEREMONY KNOWN AS MAITHUNA.

YOU WILL NEED

- *Fresh sheets and exotic bed coverings*
- *Background music*
- *Fresh flowers*
- *Aphrodisiac incense of your choice, or ylang ylang or sandalwood essential oils and oil burner*
- *Red candles*
- *Small, tempting foods that are easy to eat, perhaps finger foods, and dips*
- *Wine (in moderation)*
- *Light, flowing clothes*

METHOD

1 Your room should be spotlessly clean, with fresh sheets and exotic coverings over the bed – silks and satins are particularly sensual.

2 Play some soft music in the background, and place fresh flowers around the room.

3 Burn the incense or essential oils, and light the red candles to provide soft, sensual lighting.

4 Prepare some food in advance. Traditionally, Tantrics ate food they were not accustomed to, or foods that were taboo, in order to jolt their consciousness into a different realm. You might prefer a tray laden with small, tempting

STEP 3

Prepare a few tasty morsels to sustain you.

Fresh flowers and candles will help to set the scene.

morsels (nothing too heavy). You can add wine but in moderation, because too much alcohol dulls sexual energy.

5 Both of you should bathe and dress in light, flowing clothes.

6 First of all spend time simply enjoying each other's company, talking, eating, and drinking together. Touch and caress each other, gazing deep into each other's eyes.

7 To become aroused before intercourse, the man should meditate on the image of the vulva, what the Indians call the "yoni." Picture it as warm, welcoming, moist, and soft, opening and closing like a flower. Concentrate on the soft smell of musk and imagine the sound of a deep heartbeat, a slow rhythm of the earth, the pulse of life.

8 Meanwhile the woman should meditate on the penis, what the Indians call the "lingam." Visualize it as erect and mentally examine its different textures. The scent to imagine is patchouli; the sound is that of a faster, more insistent throb.

9 The man should now enter the woman deeply and solidly. Any position can be used, but many Tantrics prefer sitting face to face.

10 For a while just move slowly, the woman milking and the man thrusting gently.

11 Now become still, staring deep into each other's eyes. Imagine yourselves linked at the various chakras: at the head, the throat, the heart, the solar plexus, and particularly the genitals (see pages 38–39). Imagine your entire genital area surrounded by a pulsing orb of deep red light.

12 Now synchronize your breathing, slowly and deeply breathing toward your partner's mouth.

13 Imagine the energy generated from your genitals spreading up your spines and throughout your entire bodies. Stay in this position for as long as is comfortable. True Tantrics can stay like this for around thirty minutes without ejaculation, experiencing instead an almost total body orgasm. But even if you manage only a few minutes, it should still result in an unusual experience for you and your partner.

STEP 9

Tantric lovemaking can generate an intense total body orgasm.

RITUAL FOR CONCEPTION

THE MOMENT OF CONCEPTION IS AWESOME: IT IS TRUE ALCHEMY AND THE MOST PROFOUND MOMENT OF HUMAN EXISTENCE. YET ALL TOO OFTEN OUR BABIES ARE CONCEIVED WITHOUT THOUGHT OR CONSIDERATION FOR THE WONDERFUL MOMENT OF CONCEPTION. THIS LOVELY RITUAL CANNOT GUARANTEE YOU WILL CONCEIVE BUT, IF YOU ARE TRYING FOR A BABY, IT WILL ENSURE THAT YOUR CHILD HAS THE MOST PERFECT START TO ITS LIFE.

YOU WILL NEED

- *Pink or rose-colored candles*
- *Lavender and geranium oils, and oil burner*

STEP 2

Talk to each other about what you expect from parenthood.

METHOD

1 Prepare your bedroom so that it is clean and comfortable. Light the candles and burn a mixture of lavender and geranium oils, which foster love, peace, and happiness.

2 Spend some time talking with your partner. Think about why you want this baby. What can you give this child? Are you committed to providing a loving, secure environment for her or him? Be quite clear that you are not seeking a baby to support a difficult relationship or for selfish reasons.

3 Talk about your love for each other; describe how you see each other as parents. Visualize yourselves with a child of your own. How would it be?

4 Now lie down and take several slow, deep breaths. Let yourself relax completely.

5 Visualize your heart chakras (see pages 38–39) glowing with a pure golden-pink light. This light expands to become a bubble of light.

6 You gradually become aware of other bubbles of light all around you. Each one contains a soul preparing to descend to the earth to become incarnate once more.

7 Watch as some of the souls come up to you, as if they were curious. Each soul knows what she or he desires in life and is checking to see if you are able to provide the right environment.

8 Send out a prayer that the "right" soul will find you. Send out all your love, hopes, and promises. You may have a sense that a soul has picked you – if not, trust that it will happen, if not now, in the future.

9 Come back to waking awareness and share your experiences with your partner.

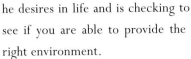

VISUALIZE THE SOUL OF THE CHILD WHO MIGHT CHOOSE YOU

Performing this conception ritual together will deepen your experience of this most intimate moment.

RELAX TOGETHER COMPLETELY

10 You could now give each other a massage (see pages 100–101) or you could perform the Maithuna ritual that is given on pages 102–103. Otherwise, if you prefer, just make love in the most gentle, caring way you can. Keep the idea of that waiting soul in your mind, quietly inviting her or him to come into your lives.

CHAPTER EIGHT

CELEBRATING THE CYCLES OF LIFE

WHEN WE RECONNECT WITH THE SACRED IN OUR EVERYDAY LIVES, WE CAN START TO SENSE THE DEEP RHYTHMS OF LIFE ONCE MORE. NATURE HAS ITS OWN GREAT YEARLY CYCLE, MOVING FROM THE DEAD OF WINTER THROUGH TO NEW LIFE IN THE SPRING; FROM FULL ABUNDANCE IN THE SUMMER TO THE SLOW DECLINE OF FALL. OUR OWN LIVES TOO, HAVE THEIR CYCLES — AND THOUGHTFUL RITUALS CAN BRING US INTO HARMONY WITH OUR SPIRITUAL AND EMOTIONAL NEEDS.

CELEBRATING THE YEAR'S CYCLE

In our modern, convenient world we often spend our lives hermetically sealed away from nature. Central heating and air-conditioning keep us cocooned from the elements, buffered from the shifting seasons. If we live in cities, we barely notice the passing of time: that subtle moment when the first snowdrops push through frozen ground; the day when summer almost imperceptibly dies and the fresh breeze of fall signals the downward shift.

Our ancestors were completely the opposite — they lived in awe of the great cycle of nature, celebrating and honoring its shifts with festivals and rituals. In this chapter we will look at simple ways of continuing the tradition of making seasonal altars and conducting ceremonies that remind us of nature's cycle, so that we can put ourselves into balance with the passing year.

MODERN RITES OF PASSAGE

Our ancestors recognized how important it was to honor the significant stages in our lives. They conducted elaborate rituals to welcome a baby into the world, and to celebrate a young person's transition from childhood to puberty. Marriage, the joining of two people, was a sacred time as well, as was the great adventure of passing from life to death. Nowadays we mark birth, marriage, and death, but often our ceremonies have lost their meaning and become trapped within rigid convention. Our rituals have become inflexible and we simply go through the motions, mouthing words and copying gestures, without experiencing the real meaning behind them. The following pages will look at how we can bring some of the magic back into our rituals and will offer suggestions to help you think about how to reinstate these ceremonies to their right and proper status.

THE CELTIC FESTIVAL YEAR

EVERY CULTURE HAS ITS SEASONAL FESTIVALS TO CELEBRATE THE PASSING YEAR. THE ANCIENT CELTIC FESTIVALS BEST ILLUSTRATE THIS BECAUSE WE STILL RETAIN VESTIGES OF THEM IN MODERN LIFE, SO MANY OF THEM WILL BE FAMILIAR. IF YOU PREFER TO FOLLOW ANY OTHER CULTURE OR RELIGION, FEEL FREE TO SUBSTITUTE CUSTOMS AND RITUALS FROM THEM. THE CELTIC YEAR IS DIVIDED INTO EIGHT PARTS, WITH A FESTIVAL ATTACHED TO EACH OF THEM.

HALLOWEEN OR SAMHAIN, OCTOBER 31

This was originally the Celtic New Year. It is a time of purification and renewal, when we think about the dark side of life – death, illness, depression – so that we can understand and learn to accept it.

HALLOWEEN ALTAR

Choose traditional symbols such as red and black candles, dried leaves, gingerbread people, pumpkins, and turnips (fashioned into lanterns if you like), pomegranates, and images of "death" goddesses – perhaps Kali might be suitable. Add photos to remind you of people you have loved who have died.

HALLOWEEN CEREMONY

Meditate on the darker side of life, accepting that life is not all bright and cheerful – there are swamplands of the soul too. You might have a Feast of the Dead: set places at the table for the dead or leave out cakes and wine for them. Divination is customary at this time of year, such as the Tarot, runes, or I Ching.

Offer cakes and wine to the dead.

Your Halloween altar should focus on the more somber aspects of life as a way of coming to terms with death and loss.

YULE, DECEMBER 21

This is the Celtic Christmas and great family festival. It is a time for the whole family to gather together, focusing on the people we need, not necessarily those we like! It is also a time to recognize that conflict has its place in life, and that we must learn how to deal with it.

The Yule log is a symbol of hope for the return of the sun.

YULE ALTAR

Evergreens such as holly, mistletoe, and ivy are traditional at this time of year. Also include bells, red and green candles, a potted tree, and gifts. You can also add family photographs, and photographs of people who cannot be with you.

YULE CEREMONY

Include fire in this ceremony because Yule is an old fire festival – the Yule log symbolizes the blazing of the newly born sun. Tie together wreaths of fir and yew to represent the old life and the new life to come. Halloween was the original Celtic "new year," but Yule took over this function many centuries ago, so this is the time to think about your resolutions for the year to come.

Yule is a time for feasting and gift-giving, for the gathering of friends and relatives in celebration.

IMBOLC AND SPRING EQUINOX

Building a seasonal altar is a simple but lovely way to honor the new energy coming into your life. Find a suitable place in your home — a table, mantelpiece, bookshelf, or even a sheltered pot in the garden — and choose suitable symbols to focus your thoughts on the lesson of the season. On these pages you will find some ideas to get you started, then just let your imagination and intuition take over.

IMBOLC, FEBRUARY 2

This is a festival of hope and trust, the time of the year when everything seems dead and yet, under the earth, new life is stirring. It is a time to focus on our dreams; it is about keeping hope alive when everything seems hopeless. It is a quiet, inward festival.

IMBOLC ALTAR

Make this altar very simple and fresh. Cover the altar with a white cloth, then add tiny candles or night lights in white or red. Add a small vase of crocuses or snowdrops. A small broom made of twigs is also customary. Write down your hopes and dreams in red ink on little pieces of white paper, then afterward bury or burn them with thanks.

A tiny twig broom is customary at Imbolc.

IMBOLC CEREMONY

As it gets dark, sit and meditate, giving thanks for the knowledge that life will spring again. Once it is dark, light tiny candles, one by one, until the room is full of light – this represents the return of the Goddess. Give each other, and particularly children, little gifts symbolizing the small hopes that sustain us through tough times.

The Imbolc altar has fresh flowers and is flooded with the light of hope and rebirth.

SPRING EQUINOX, MARCH 21

This festival equates with our modern Easter and celebrates the return of life. This is the time to do spring cleaning, both physically and emotionally. It is a time to get rid of whatever has stuck to you in the winter – things and people you have outgrown.

The Spring Equinox marks the return of the Goddess after the deathly winter.

SPRING EQUINOX ALTAR

A joyful altar full of spring flowers, pussy willow, or other buds. Eggs are traditional – paint or dye them with natural colorings. Hares are an old Easter symbol, and you can also add some hot cross buns. Choose green candles to light the altar.

SPRING CEREMONY

Celebrate this festival at either dawn or dusk, the in-between times of the day. You might like to include planting seeds – physical ones in the ground and spiritual ones in your rituals.

What do you need for this coming year? Love, friendship, wisdom, understanding? Light fresh green candles to confirm your desires, or paint your wishes on eggs that can be boiled and eaten.

Decorated eggs are traditional at the Spring Equinox.

The symbolism of the Spring Equinox altar represents new life and new beginnings.

BELTANE AND SUMMER SOLSTICE

How you celebrate the passing seasons is totally up to you. By using the ideas and symbolism given on the previous pages, you may well find you can come up with rituals that feel right for you. On these pages there are a few suggestions for the kind of ceremonies that might be appropriate. Use them as inspiration only, then adapt them as you wish. These rituals should be completely your own.

BELTANE, MAY 1

Also celebrated as May Day, this is a life-affirming festival of sex, energy, and freedom. It is one of the great fire festivals and a traditional time for engagements and marriages. It symbolizes the fresh new energy of spring that is wild and untamed.

BELTANE ALTAR

Make your altar as exuberant and colorful as possible: start with garlands of blossoms, greenery and flowers, and add brightly colored streamers. Statues of the Celtic God and Goddess are

appropriate, or you could choose deities from your preferred religion. You could also make a tiny maypole or place a drum on the altar.

Celebrate Beltane with music.

BELTANE CEREMONY

Build a bonfire or make a ring of candles in storm lanterns. Beat drums and make music. Dress in green flowing robes or, if you have the nerve, go bare-fleshed – and dance! A May Cup of white wine, strawberries, and sweet woodruff, decorated with edible flowers such as chives and borage, is the ideal drink. There is no need for pompous ceremony here, so just have fun.

Beltane is a time for exuberance, color, feasting, and dancing around the maypole.

SUMMER SOLSTICE, JUNE 21

This is the time to gather together in large groups – it is all about learning your place in society and the world. It is a time to examine what you want from life and to look at who you really are. It is usually celebrated as a great party.

SUMMER ALTAR

Make your altar predominantly red – a red cloth perhaps, and red candles. Now add heaps of summer fruits, roses, larkspur, and heather. If you have access to them, include magical midsummer herbs such as mugwort, vervain, St. John's wort, and thyme.

SUMMER CEREMONY

Make images of the sun and hang them in a nearby tree to protect your home. Light a midsummer fire – traditionally made of pine and oak – and celebrate around it. Get together with friends for an outdoor picnic, a barbecue on the beach, or an all-night party on top of a hill. Tell your friends how much you appreciate them and enjoy their company.

Stonehenge in England is a dramatic witness to the ancient importance of Midsummer.

Feast with your friends under the sky to celebrate the summer sun.

The vivid red of the Summer Solstice altar represents the fiery Midsummer sun.

LAMMAS AND AUTUMN EQUINOX

BUILDING A SEASONAL ALTAR IS VERY MUCH A MATTER OF INDIVIDUAL CHOICE, SO READERS OUTSIDE THE CELTIC LANDS SHOULD NOT WORRY IF THEY CANNOT GET SOME OF THE FLOWERS, FRUITS, VEGETABLES, HERBS, OR OTHER ITEMS SUGGESTED ON THESE PAGES. JUST REPLACE THEM WITH WHATEVER SEASONAL ITEMS ARE AVAILABLE IN YOUR OWN COUNTRY. YOU CAN ALSO USE IDEAS FROM ANY OF YOUR OWN SEASONAL FESTIVALS — LET YOUR INTUITION BE YOUR GUIDE.

LAMMAS, AUGUST 1

This is the great thanksgiving festival that is often celebrated as Harvest Festival. At this time of year we recognize that we all have to kill in order to live and we should give thanks to the plants and animals that give their life to nourish us. It is also a time to think about what we can give back to the world.

Lammas is a time of thanksgiving for the gifts of nature.

LAMMAS ALTAR

Gold is the predominant color here: use a yellow cloth and yellow candles. Add fruits and vegetables, cobs of corn, and loaves of bread. You could make necklaces from seeds, "dollies" from grain, or bake dough figures of the Celtic Mother Goddess or other fertility goddess. Write little notes of thanks on gold or yellow slips of paper to people who have helped you, then give the notes to them, or bury or burn them with thanks.

Grain dolly

LAMMAS CEREMONY

This is a thanksgiving ceremony – especially for food. Bake bread and knead in your thanks; make grain dollies or bread figures of the Mother Goddess or other fertility goddess, and charge them with your hopes and wishes; have a family feast of thanks.

AUTUMN EQUINOX, SEPTEMBER 21

This is a purification festival, honoring the departure of the Earth Goddess, and preparing for the coming of winter and the dark months ahead. This is a time for quiet, inward work, when we let go of those parts of us that no longer serve us.

AUTUMN EQUINOX ALTAR

Choose the rich russet colors of autumn/fall: burnt oranges, deep reds, rusty yellows, darker greens. Make wreaths of oak leaves and nuts. Add pumpkins, apples, pine cones, and dried herbs. Choose yellow candles for the altar.

The Autumn Equinox is a time of gathering in and preparing ourselves for the rigors of winter.

AUTUMN EQUINOX CEREMONY

Collect seeds from the flowers and vegetables in your garden, and whisper into the seeds your hope for the life that will stay dormant until next spring. Prepare yourself for the winter by doing all the small tasks such as mending sweaters, putting away summer clothes, painting your house, and turn your thoughts inward as you do them.

Mending winter clothes is a good ceremony for the Autumn Equinox.

The russet colors of the Autumn Equinox altar remind us of the turning of the year.

RITES OF PASSAGE: BIRTH

THE BIRTH OF A NEW BABY IS A MIRACLE. AFTER NINE MONTHS OF FLOATING IN THE WOMB, A NEW PERSON HAS ARRIVED TO TAKE HIS OR HER PLACE IN THE WORLD. THIS BIRTH RITUAL CALLS ON THE POWER OF THE ELEMENTS — FIRE, AIR, WATER, AND EARTH — TO WELCOME, LOVE, AND PROTECT THE NEW CHILD. IT IS ALSO A TIME FOR SHARING YOUR JOY WITH OTHER LOVED ONES, AND IT GIVES THEM AN OPPORTUNITY TO WELCOME THE NEW BABY INTO THE WORLD.

YOU WILL NEED

◆ *A white candle*

◆ *Rose or lavender oil, and oil burner*

◆ *A bowl of water (spring water is ideal)*

◆ *A crystal (rose quartz is perfect — leave it in salt water for 72 hours to cleanse it before this ceremony)*

◆ *Colored cotton or embroidery thread*

METHOD

1 The mother should hold the baby while everyone gathers around. If it is possible, try to hold this ritual outside.

2 Hold the baby up to the sky, saying: "This child has come from the world of spirit. Let her/his spirit soar free and happy in this life."

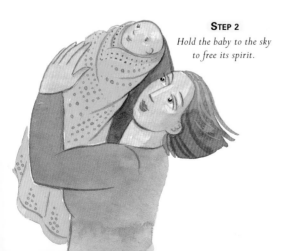

STEP 2
Hold the baby to the sky to free its spirit.

3 Now place the baby on the earth, saying: "This is a child of the earth. May she/he feel at home and secure in this world."

STEP 3
Offer the baby the security of the earth.

4 Light the candle and oil burner (you may need to enclose them in glass jars without the lids to keep them alight). Add four drops of rose or lavender oil to the water reservoir and take in the sweet, loving scent.

5 Hold up the lighted candle and say aloud: "May the Spirit of Fire give this child strength and courage."

STEP 5
Give the baby the strength of fire.

6 Hold up the oil burner and say: "May the Spirit of Air give this child farsightedness and vision."

7 Hold up the bowl of water and anoint the child on the forehead, throat, heart, solar plexus, and genitals, and say: "May the Spirit of Water give this child love, warmth, and happiness."

8 Hold up the crystal to the child's heart and say: "May the Spirit of Earth give this child confidence, self-esteem, and self-assurance to walk firmly, without fear, in the world."

9 Now everyone should take a strand of cotton or thread. Take it in turns to come up to the child and give him or her a cuddle, a touch, or a kiss. Give the child a blessing and a wish for a positive quality or characteristic. As you give your wish, place your thread around the child's wrist and attach the ends loosely in a single tie.

10 After the ceremony, the threads can be braided together and made into an amulet to be kept in the child's room or carriage, but out of the child's reach.

STEP 9

Each person present can tie a thread around the baby's wrist as a token of blessing.

STEP 10

Braid the threads together to collect the blessings.

RITES OF PASSAGE: PUBERTY

PUBERTY CAN BE A DIFFICULT TIME. IT SIGNALS STEPPING OVER THE THRESHOLD FROM CHILDHOOD TO THE FIRST STAGES OF ADULTHOOD. DEEPLY SIGNIFICANT FOR BOTH BOYS AND GIRLS, IT IS AN IMPORTANT TIME OF TRANSITION. UNLIKE OUR ANCESTORS, HOWEVER, WE RARELY MARK OR CELEBRATE THE ARRIVAL OF PUBERTY. THIS RITUAL MAY HELP TO EASE THE CONFUSION THAT OFTEN ACCOMPANIES THIS TIME, BUT MAKE SURE THAT THE YOUNG PERSON LIKES AND APPROVES OF THE IDEA.

YOU WILL NEED

- *Something that symbolizes childhood for the adolescent*
- *Something that symbolizes the young person's hopes for the future*
- *A curtain or archway, or a door between two rooms*
- *Presents (optional)*

METHOD

1 The adolescent should choose something symbolic of childhood, a favorite toy or teddy bear perhaps. Also choose something that represents his or her hopes for the future, for the adult life to come – this could be a pen and paper, something from the natural world, a football, or a riding hat perhaps. The choice should be left to the child.

STEP 1
Let the young person choose symbols of the childhood that is past and of the adult life to come.

STEP 2
All those present can share memories of the young person's childhood.

2 The young person holds on to the childhood symbol and sits on the floor. The adults gather together, seated on chairs, in a circle around the

118

adolescent. The soon-to-be adult might want to talk about childhood, about what was good and bad about it. The surrounding people, family and perhaps friends, can also give recollections.

STEP 3
Taking the young person to a doorway represents the passage into adulthood.

3 Next an older member of the family (ideally of the same sex as the adolescent) should act as guardian, taking the young person's hand and leading him or her to the threshold (curtain, archway, or door). Standing on the threshold, the guardian asks the adolescent if he or she has any fears or concerns about growing-up. The adolescent should voice any fears and everyone should acknowledge them.

4 The guardian now hands the young person the chosen symbol of adulthood, calling on the Spirits or a guardian angel to take him or her safely over this important threshold of life.

5 Then the guardian steps back and the adolescent walks through the gateway, affirming: "I now step from childhood into the gateway of adulthood. Protect me, help me, make me brave, firm, and strong."

6 The young person may choose to spend some time in quiet meditation at this point.

7 After this, the new adult returns to the room and takes a place in the circle, this time sitting on a chair with the adults. This is a good time to let the adolescent talk about any worries, concerns, or doubts he or she may have about growing up. Everyone could give a small present. Or you could share a meal, and perhaps give the young adult his or her first glass of wine.

STEP 7
At the end of the ceremony, the young person joins the adults.

119

RITES OF PASSAGE: MARRIAGE OR BONDING

When we celebrate marriage in today's society, the meaning of the ceremony is often lost amid the sumptuous catering, expensive gifts, and elaborate preparations. At its heart, a marriage is simply a way of two people dedicating themselves to each other, promising to share their lives and love while retaining their own identities. This ceremony helps to focus on that profound truth.

YOU WILL NEED

- *Enough stones to make a circle large enough for 2 people and an altar*
- *Flowers, greenery, and petals to suit the occasion*
- *God and Goddess figures (see below), optional*
- *A green cloth*
- *3 candles: one pink, one orange, and one red*
- *Rose and neroli essential oils, and oil burner*

METHOD

1 If you can, hold this ceremony outside. Make a circle out of the stones. You could construct an arch over the circle, laden with greenery and flowers. If family and friends are present, they should stand outside the circle.

2 Place the other items on your altar within the stones: a green cloth over the altar, perhaps figures of the God and Goddess from your chosen culture, and flowers and petals. One candle should be in the center of the altar, the others on either side.

3 Light the burner and add one drop each of rose and neroli oils to the water reservoir. Their delicious scents are singular, yet meld together to create a divine perfume – a good symbol for your marriage.

4 Each partner now takes a candle from the altar, lights it, and stands outside the circle.

5 Take it in turns to state who you are, what you hold dear in life, and what you love about this person you have chosen to be your partner. State that you accept that you are both individuals with your own lives, and that you promise never to threaten that independence.

6 Now hold hands and walk together into the circle. Stand before the altar and together light the single candle from the wicks of your individual candles. Place your individual candles at either side of the altar.

7 As the central candle flame grows stronger, recognize that this will be the strength of your love – you are separate people who are important in your own right, but together you are more than the sum of your two parts. Acknowledge the mystery of love.

8 Now make your commitment to each other — the words should be personal and, if you like, private. You might want to exchange rings or other pieces of circular jewelry as symbols of eternity, or give each other gifts. A kiss is customary at this point.

9 Hold hands, and then walk out of the circle together. This is the time when any other people present can shower you with petals and their blessings and good wishes for the future. Now enjoy a feast with plenty of music and dancing.

A simple ritual of dedication within a sacred space can be as meaningful as the most extravagant ceremony.

RITES OF PASSAGE: DEATH AND REMEMBRANCE

DEATH IS THE GREAT BUGBEAR OF OUR SOCIETY. WE FEAR DEATH SO MUCH IT HAS BECOME SOMETHING WE TRY TO DENY OR FORGET; WE TEND TO PUSH IT TO THE BACK OF OUR MINDS AND TRY TO FORGET THAT IT WILL, ONE DAY, COME TO ALL OF US. MODERN FUNERALS ARE SOMBER, GRIM AFFAIRS THAT RARELY BRING COMFORT. THIS CEREMONY HELPS TO PUT DEATH IN ITS TRUE CONTEXT — SIMPLY AS ANOTHER VITAL STAGE OF LIFE.

YOU WILL NEED

- *Sandalwood and juniper essential oils, and oil burner*
- *Homeopathic ignatia tablets*
- *Photographs and remembrances of the person who has died*
- *Candles*

METHOD

1 Light the oil burner and add three drops each of sandalwood and juniper oils. Sandalwood helps to mark transitions, while juniper supports the spirit in difficult times.

2 Everyone should gather together in a circle. You may wish to sing a song or play a piece of music that reminds you of the person who has died. Don't worry if the tears start – allowing the grief to pour out is part of the healing process. If anyone finds the sorrow too much, offer a tablet of ignatia, the homeopathic remedy for intense grief.

3 Anyone who wishes should place a photo, or other reminder of the person, in the center of the circle. Use this time to remember him or her: recount old tales, memories, silly stories. Talk about what the person meant to you – the bad as well as the good. No one is perfect.

4 When everyone has finished, lie down on your backs with your heads pointing into the center of the circle. Join hands loosely if you like. Relax and pay attention to your breathing. Allow yourselves several minutes to calm both body and mind.

5 Now visualize your heart chakra (see page 39), pulsing with love for the dead person. Then visualize your heart chakra joining together with those of the others to create a large shimmering bubble of beautiful pink-gold light.

6 See in the center of the bubble the person who has died. Send him or her all your love. Say anything you feel was left unsaid, either aloud or silently. You may feel that the person has a message for you.

7 Now accept that it is time to let the person move on. Cut the ties that hold him or her to you and to the earth, and let the person go with unconditional love.

8 Watch as the person seems to rise up through the bubble of light and moves into another bubble – an immense embracing sea of pure, white light.

The person seems happy to leave now, knowing that you accept it. Imagine yourself waving goodbye, knowing that you will meet again.

9 Come back to normal waking consciousness and share your experiences with the others. You may want to continue in quiet meditation, or you may wish to join together to eat and drink. If you prefer, you could make it into a celebration of the person's life – if you do so, don't be afraid to laugh, tell jokes, and remember that person with joy.

Bring those who have died into the circle of the friends who loved them and create a safe space to let them go.

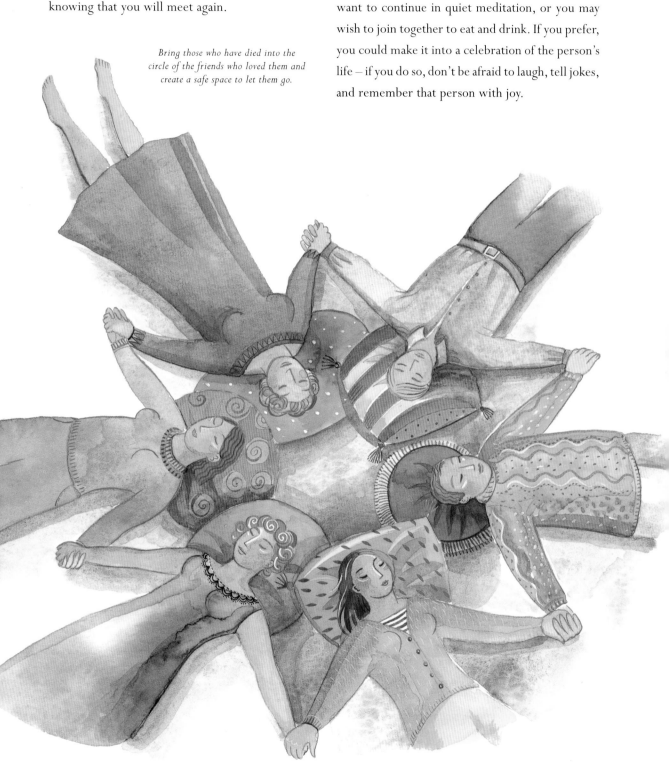

SACRED GATHERINGS
WITH FRIENDS

MEETING UP WITH FRIENDS IS ONE OF THE GREAT JOYS OF LIFE. WHILE NOBODY WOULD SUGGEST THAT YOU SHOULD TURN EACH MEETING INTO AN INTENSE RITUAL, THESE HAPPY MEETINGS CAN PROVIDE WONDERFUL OPPORTUNITIES FOR BRINGING SACREDNESS INTO YOUR EVERYDAY LIFE AND SHOWING YOUR APPRECIATION TO YOUR FRIENDS. THESE PAGES OFFER A FEW SUGGESTIONS ON HOW TO MAKE GATHERINGS WITH YOUR FRIENDS SACRED AND FUN.

SHOW YOUR APPRECIATION

Friends are special but we rarely take the opportunity to show how much we love and appreciate them. Try these suggestions or invent some of your own:

Children are reassured by familiar rituals.

• Take your friend a small gift – a card, a poem, a posy of flowers, a tape of special music – as a token of your love, friendship, and appreciation.

• When you share a meal together, spend a few moments before eating to mention some of the reasons why you are so fond of your friend. Think of it as a form of grace.

• If a friend is feeling low, suggest you have a "talk-it-out" session – a chance for the friend to talk and for you to listen. Only make suggestions if your friend is happy for you to do so. Otherwise just be there for him or her and be ready to offer your support.

• Think of activities your friend would enjoy. Surprise your friend by suggesting a visit to an art gallery, a concert, a picnic in the park – they may not be your favorite activities, but be selfless and think of what your friend might like.

ENJOY THE OUTDOORS

We rarely spend enough time in nature. Getting together with friends is the perfect opportunity to enjoy the elements and to have fun, that essential ingredient of sacred living.

- What did you most enjoy as children? Go skinny-dipping in a pond, play hide and seek, go ice-skating, or horseback riding. Play imaginary games.
- Eat outside. Get together for picnics in the park, or barbecues on the beach. If it's cold, wrap up warm and huddle around a fire, eating baked potatoes, and drinking hot soup.
- Children love nature. If you have children, arrange a meeting with friends who have children of similar ages to yours, and then encourage their interest and excitement by sending them on treasure hunts. Ask them to find a natural object for each letter of the alphabet. Teach them to recognize trees, plants, flowers, and animal footprints.
- Honor a sacred place. Visit a known sacred place or choose your own and bring it offerings: a garland of flowers, an inscribed stone, perhaps a carved piece of wood. Send your love, good wishes, and blessing to the spirit of the place.

Even watching a movie together can be transformed into a sacred occasion.

HOME PLEASURES

When you are stuck in the house, it doesn't mean you can't enjoy the sacred. Try these suggestions:
- Make a meal together: pretend you are cooking a magical meal in a sacred caldron and invest your cooking with all your hopes and dreams.
- Bake bread together: kneading is therapeutic and watching bread rise is quite magical. Create your own weird and wonderful shapes.
- Have an afternoon watching your favorite inspirational movies together – with popcorn, ice cream, and soda of course. Talk about why the movies resonate with you so much.
- Spend a day in silent retreat with your friends. Fill the day with meditation, peace, and shared food and drink in friendly silence.
- Get together to practice yoga, to listen to a visualization tape, or perhaps to try some of the rituals in this book.

Share the pleasures of the great outdoors with your family.

INDEX

INDEX

USEFUL ADDRESSES

AROMATHERAPY
Natura Trading Ltd.
Box 263
1857 West 4th Avenue
Vancouver B.C. V63 1M4
Canada
Tel: 1 604 732 7531

BACH FLOWER REMEDIES
(GREAT BRITAIN)
Dr. Edward Bach Centre
Mount Vernon, Sotwell
Wallingford
Oxon OX10 0PZ
Great Britain
Tel: 44 1491 834678

BACH FLOWER REMEDIES
(AUSTRALIA)
Martin & Pleasance
137 Swan Street, Richmond
Victoria 3121
Australia
Tel: 61 39 427 7422

BACH FLOWER REMEDIES
(USA)
Nelson Bach USA Ltd.
Wilmington Technology Park
100 Research Drive, Wilmington
Massachusetts 01887–4406
USA
Tel: 1 508 988 3833

HOMEOPATHY
American Institute of
  Homeopathy
1585 Glencoe Street, Suite 44
Denver, Colorado 80220–1338
USA
Tel: 1 303 321 4105

KIRLIAN (AURA) PHOTOGRAPHY
Guy Mason
4 Greenfields,
Nyewood
Petersfield
Hampshire GU31 5JH
Great Britain
Tel: 44 1730 821690

ACKNOWLEDGMENTS

PICTURE CREDITS

The author and publishers are grateful to the following
for permission to reproduce illustrations:

AKG Photo pp.24r, 93, 95r

Bridgeman Art Library pp.94, 95l

Eye Ubiquitous pp.45, 48–9

Fortean Picture Library p.113t

Image Bank pp.13tr, 15, 27, 30l, 57, 65, 80, 115t

Images p.111tl

Stock Market pp.6, 8t and b, 9bl, 10t and b, 12t, 25tr, 28l, 58 (circle), 60
81 (main picture), 83, 107, 113c, 124l , 124–5, 125t

Harry Smith Collection p.41 (all main pictures)

Sarah Young pp.16, 17 (all), 23 (all), 37b, 62, 63, 74, 75 (all), 84t and b, 85 (all), 86t and b,
87l and r, 97, 104, 105 (all), 116 (all), 117 (all), 118l and r, 119 (all), 121, 123

THANKS ALSO TO
Harveys Furnishing Group Ltd.
Hanningtons of Brighton